STEP BY STEP APPROACH TO ENGLISH CONVERSATION

STEP BY STEP APPROACH TO ENGLISH CONVERSATION

by

Madan Sood

M.A. English (Lit.)

Formerly of Indian Air Force

Published by :
GOODWILL PUBLISHING HOUSE
B-3, Rattan Jyoti, 18, Rajendra Place,
New Delhi-110008 (INDIA)
Ph. : 25750801, 25820556
Fax : 91-11-25764396
Web : goodwillpublishinghouse.com
E-mail : goodwillpub@vsnl.net

Laser Typeset at : Computer Corner, New Delhi

Printed at : Kumar Offset Printers, Delhi-92

PREFACE

How you can best improve your spoken English depends on where you live and particularly on whether or not you live in English speaking community. If you hear English spoken everyday and mix freely with English speaking people, that on the whole, is an advantage. On the other hand, it is often confusing to have the whole language poured over you at once.

A child learns his mother tongue even without learning, reading and writing and he does so by listening to the people around and then he starts speaking. This child is not aware of any grammar nor does he know any other rules. This is how naturally a child learns a language—his mother tongue. The role of listening is, therefore, very important in learning a spoken language. A grown-up person who wants to learn English, should also, first begin with listening. If one does not understand what others speak in English, one cannot converse with them in English. Besides being a good listener, one should associate with people who mostly speak in English. Also, one should listen more to radio-broadcasts, interviews, quizzes etc.

There is no denying the fact that one may be a good writer and a good reader also, but he may not be able to speak fluently. Some people are of the view that, 'the more the command over written English, the more the command over spoken English'. On the other hand, some hold the view that the world of spoken English is far different from that of written English.

Though there may be some truth in both these opinions, the fact cannot be denied that after one has learnt to speak some English, one must master the rules of grammar so that one can speak and write flawlessly, otherwise, the basic objective of speaking or writing accurate English shall remain defeated and hence the inevitability of acquainting oneself with grammar.

Step by Step Approach to English Conversation acquaints the learner with the rules of basic grammar and proceeds with exercises on questions-answers and conversation.

Apart from school and college students and students preparing for some competitive examination/interview, any learner of any age belonging to any walk of life can derive maximum benefit from this book as it ensures that the whole language is not poured over the learner at once but he is made to learn, grasp and assimilate a few rules and then the subsequent rules are explained so that he can follow the same process, thereby gaining slowly but surely.

— Madan Sood

CONTENTS

Chapter 1 Alphabet

There are 26 letters in English Alphabet

A, B, C, D, E, F, G, H, I, J, K, L, M, N, O, P, Q, R, S, T, U, V, W, X, Y, Z.

English Alphabet is divided into:

5	Vowels	a, e, i, o, u
21	Consonants	b, c, d, f, g, h, j, k, l, m, n, p, q, r, s, t, v, w, x, y, z.

Sl.No.	Capital Letters	Small letters
1.	A	a
2.	B	b
3.	C	c
4.	D	d
5.	E	e
6.	F	f
7.	G	g
8.	H	h
9.	I	i
10.	J	j
11.	K	k
12.	L	l
13.	M	m
14.	N	n

15.	**O**	**o**
16.	**P**	**p**
17.	**Q**	**q**
18.	**R**	**r**
19.	**S**	**s**
20.	**T**	**t**
21.	**U**	**u**
22.	**V**	**v**
23.	**W**	**w**
24.	**X**	**x**
25.	**Y**	**y**
26.	**Z**	**z**

A, AN, THE

'A', **'an'** and **'the'** are called Articles. **A or an** is called the *indefinite Article*. **'The'** is called the *Definite Article*

Before a word beginning with a vowel sound, 'an' is, used; as;

an ass
an ice cream
an apple
an egg
an inkstand
an hour
an honest man
an owl
an umbrella

Before a word beginning with a consonant sound 'a' is used; as,

a boy
a woman
a horse
a hole
a ball
a cat
a doll
a fan
a book
a house
a crow
a girl
a kite
a pen
a table
a van

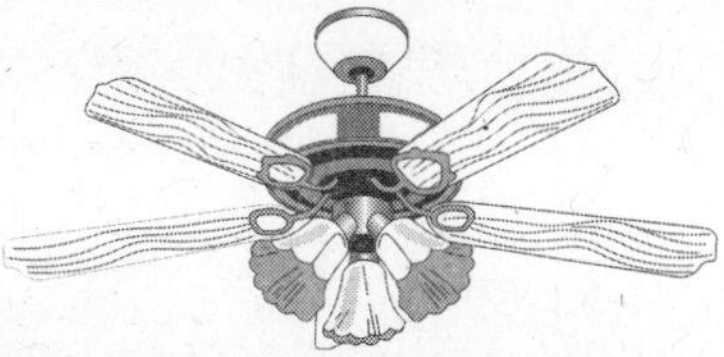

Note:

an hour, an honest man

'An' is used before **'hour'** and **'honest'** because they give a *vowel* sound.

a University
a Union
a European

'A' is used before 'university', 'union' and 'European' because they give a ***consonant*** sound.

'The' is used with singular and plural words and can be used before ***vowels*** and ***consonants***.

the boy	the boys
the woman	the women
the horse	the horses
the ball	the balls
the cat	the cats
the doll	the dolls
the fan	the fans
the kite	the kites
the lamp	the lamps
the pen	the pens

'The' is also used

(i) when a particular person or thing is spoken of; as,

I know *the* way.

Can you give him *the* message?

(ii) When a particular thing or person has already been referred to, as,

The present you gave me is very beautiful.

(iii) With the names of rivers, seas, oceans, gulfs, group of islands and mountain ranges; as,

The Ganges

The Alps

The Red Sea

(iv) Before the names of holy books; as

The Gita

The Bible

The Quran

(v) Before newspapers, magazines

The London Times

The Times of India

The Sun

(vi) Before

the earth

the sky

the moon

the sun

(vii) Before musical instruments, as

I can play *the* guitar.

EXERCISE-1

Make words with the following letters:

1. oyb ____________
2. nawom ____________
3. oleh ____________
4. tac ____________
5. nfa ____________
6. lppea ____________
7. lalb ____________
8. dgo ____________
9. geg ____________
10. edb ____________

EXERCISE-2

Fill in the blanks with 'a', 'an', or 'the'.

1. He is _________ good boy.
2. I have lost _________ pen which you gave me.
3. Darcy is _________ honest girl.
4. There is _________ inkpot on the table.
5. I waited for you for _________ hour.
6. She is _________ honorable woman.
7. I met _________ European in the party.
8. How beautiful _________ sky looks!
9. Gold is _________ precious metal.
10. He has come without _________ umbrella.

SHAPES

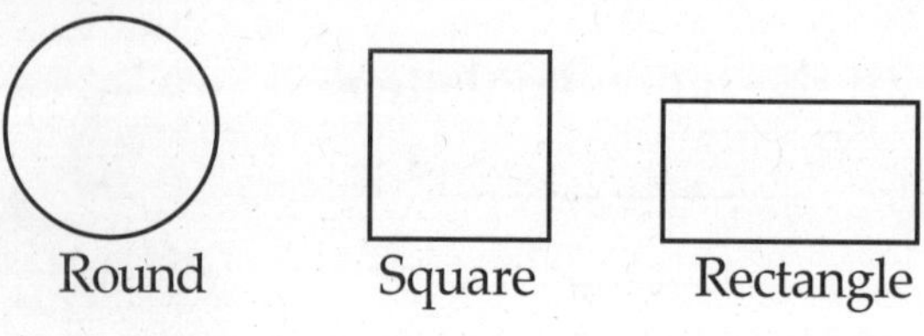

Round Square Rectangle

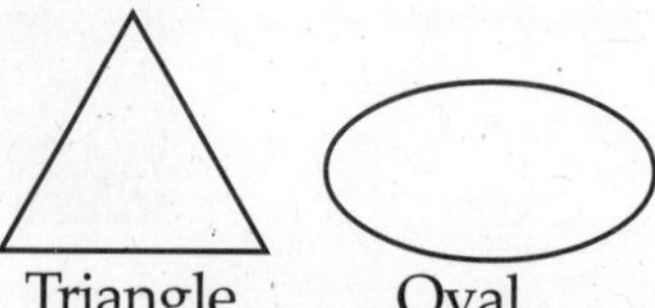

Triangle Oval

1. This is a round table.
2. A square has four equal sides.
3. The drawing room is rectangular.
4. This kite is triangular.
5. An egg is oval.

Cardinal Number		Ordinal Number	
Words	**Figures**		
One	1	First	1st
Two	2	second	2nd
Three	3	third	3rd
Four	4	fourth	4th
Five	5	fifth	5th
Six	6	sixth	6th
Seven	7	seventh	7th
Eight	8	eighth	8th
Nine	9	ninth	9th
Ten	10	tenth	10th
Eleven	11	eleventh	11th
Twelve	12	twelfth	12th
Thirteen	13	thirteenth	13th
Fourteen	14	fourteenth	14th
Fifteen	15	fifteenth	15th
Sixteen	16	sixteenth	16th
Seventeen	17	seventeenth	17th
Eighteen	18	eighteenth	18th
Nineteen	19	nineteenth	19th
Twenty	20	twentieth	20th
Twenty one	21	twenty first	21st
Twenty two	22	twenty second	22nd
Twenty three	23	twenty third	23rd

Twenty four	24	twenty fourth	24th
Twenty five	25	twenty fifth	25th
Twenty six	26	twenty sixth	26th
Twenty seven	27	twenty seventh	27th
Twenty eight	28	twenty eighth	28th
Twenty nine	29	twenty ninth	29th
Thirty	30	thirtieth	30th
Thirty one	31	thirty first	31st
Thirty two	32	thirty second	32nd
Thirty three	33	thirty third	33rd
Thirty four	34	thirty fourth	34th
Thirty five	35	thirty fifth	35th
Thirty six	36	thirty sixth	36th
Thirty seven	37	thirty seventh	37th
Thirty eight	38	thirty eighth	38th
Thirty nine	39	thirty ninth	39th
Forty	40	fortieth	40th
Forty one	41	forty first	41st
Forty two	42	forth second	42nd
Forty three	43	forty third	43rd
Forty four	44	forty fourth	44th
Forty five	45	forty fifth	45th
Forty six	46	forty sixth	46th
Forty seven	47	forty seventh	47th
Forty eight	48	forty eighth	48th

Forty nine	49	forty ninth	49th
Fifty	50	fiftieth	50th
Sixty	60	sixtieth	60th
Seventy	70	seventieth	70th
Eighty	80	eightieth	80th
Ninety	90	ninetieth	90th
One hundred	100	one hundredth	100th

Chapter 2 The Sentence

When we speak or write we use **words**. We generally use these words in groups; as,

Little Jack Horner sat in a corner.

A group of words like this, which makes complete sense, is called a ***sentence***; as,

(i) I go to school everyday.

(ii) She met me in the market.

(iii) My mother cooks food daily.

KINDS OF SENTENCES

Sentences are of five kinds:-

Assertive or Declarative:

Such sentences make statement; as,

They play cricket on Sundays.

Interrogative:

These are questions; as

Have you done your home work?

Imperative:

They express command, request or order, as

Don't make a noise.

Please come here.

Exclamatory:

These sentences express sudden feelings of joy, sorrow or surprise; as,

Alas! Her only son is dead.

What a wonderful weather!

Optative:

They express a wish; as

May you live long!

EXERCISE 3

Fill in the blanks with Assertive, Interrogative, Imperative, Exclamatory or Optative:

1. The tiger is in the cage. __________

2. Please bring a glass of water. __________
3. Don't make a noise. __________
4. May you be blessed with a son! __________
5. Hurrah! we have won the series! __________
6. Alas! her only son is dead. __________
7. Listen to the speech attentively. __________
8. Where do you live? __________

9. He is plucking flowers. ___________

10. He goes to office everyday. ___________
11. He has returned my books. ___________
12. The child has been crying since morning. ___________
13. The brave soldier lost an arm in the battle. ___________
14. Show me your home work. ___________
15. Where are you going? ___________
16. Do not violate the rules. ___________
17. May you live long! ___________
18. Do you play cricket? ___________

19. Where has he gone? ___________

20. What a wonderful weather! __________

21. She can solve these sums. __________
22. I was treated well by all. __________
23. Lift this box. __________

24. Come here. __________
25. What a shameful act! __________

Chapter 3 Subject and Predicate

Every sentence has two parts.

The part which names the person or thing we are speaking about, is called the ***Subject*** of the sentence.

The part which tells something about the subject, is called the ***Predicate*** of the sentence.

Note: Verb is the part of the Predicate.

Study the following sentence:

(i) He came here yesterday.

(ii) We shall meet you tomorrow.

(iii) Getting up early can keep you fit.

In sentence (i) **'He'** is the ***subject*** and the remaining part of the sentence **came here yesterday** is the ***predicate***.

In sentence (ii) **'We'** is the ***subject*** and '**shall meet you tomorrow**' is the ***predicate***.

In sentence (iii) '**Getting up early**' is the ***subject*** and '**can keep you fit**' is the ***predicate***.

The ***subject*** of a sentence generally comes first but it can also be used after the ***predicate***; as,

(i) On the hill sat the saint meditating.

(ii) Towers falling, he saw.

Note: In Imperative sentences, the subject is understood and hence not used; as,

Come here (Here the subject 'you' is understood).

EXERCISE 4

Supply the subjects in the following sentences:

1. __________ have seen this movie.
2. __________ is making tea.
3. __________ know him.
4. __________ fly kites on the Republic Day.
5. __________ has washed the clothes.
6. __________ heard a barking sound.
7. __________ sat on the hill.
8. __________ have completed their home work.

EXERCISE 5

Supply the Predicates in the following sentences:

1. The hunter __________
2. My father __________
3. The French Army __________
4. Practice and experience __________
5. He __________
6. The peon __________
7. The children __________
8. Manners __________

Chapter 4 The Phrase and the Clause

PHRASE

A ***phrase*** is a group of words which does not have a subject and predicate and which does not make complete sense; as,

In the corner

With black hair

In the beginning

In a polite manner.

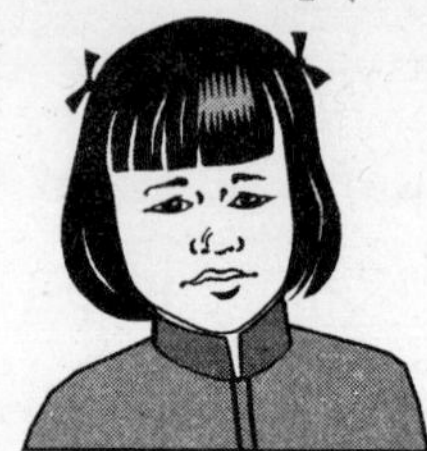

The above group of words *'in the corner'*, *'with black hair'* *'in the beginning'* and *'in a polite manner'* are the ***phrases*** because they don't have subjects and predicates and they don't make a complete sense.

CLAUSE

A ***clause*** is a group of words which has its own subject and predicate, but it does not make a complete sense; as,

When I was working

If you work hard

That he will come

All the above three are clauses because they have their own subject and predicate but they do not make a complete sense.

EXERCISE 6

Separate the sentences, clauses and phrases in the following:

1. That he will come in time. ______________
2. If they had reached there. ______________
3. All are born to suffer. ______________
4. Man is mortal. ______________
5. In the air. ______________
6. To learn driving. ______________
7. Although he is rich. ______________
8. With a long tail. ______________
9. To carry out the work. ______________
10. He climbed. ______________

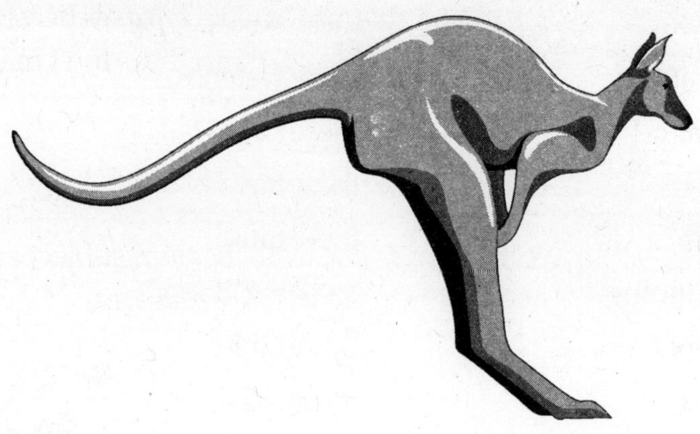

Chapter 5 This, That, These, Those, Is, Are

THIS, THAT, THESE, THOSE:

'This' and **'that'** are used with ***singular words***.

'These' and **'those'** are used with ***plural words***.

'This' and **'these'** are used for things which are close to us.

'That' and **'those'** are used for things which are far away from us.

Singular (Close by)	**Plural (Close by)**
This mango	these mangoes
This box	these boxes
This watch	these watches
This bat	these bats
This boy	these boys
This fan	these fans
This building	these buildings.
This table	these tables
This jug	these jugs
This van	these vans

Singular (far away)	**Plural (far away)**
That mango	those mangoes
That box	those boxes
That watch	those watches

That bat	those bats
That boy	those boys
That fan	those fans
That building	those buildings
That table	those tables
That jug	those jugs
That van	those vans

Antonyms (Opposites)

fat	thin
big	small
high	low
tall	short
success	failure
strength	weakness
regular	irregular
suitable	unsuitable
weak	strong
courteous	discourteous

IS AND ARE

'Is' is used with 'this' and 'that'. 'Are' is used with 'these' and 'those'.

This is a mango	These are mangoes
This is a box	these are boxes
This is a watch	these are watches
This is a bat	these are bats

This is a boy these are boys
This is a fan these are fans
This is a building these are buildings
This is a table these are tables
This is a jug these are jugs
This is a van these are vans.

EXERCISE 7

Provide singular and plural words in the following:

This ____________ these ____________

This ____________ these ____________

This ____________ these ____________

This ____________ these ____________

This ____________ these ____________

EXERCISE 8

Provide 'this' and 'these' in the following sentences:

____________ ball ____________ balls

____________ house ____________ houses

____________ apple ____________ apples

____________ girl ____________ girls

____________ pen ____________ pens

____________ table ____________ tables

Chapter 6

Parts of Speech

The words are divided into different kinds according to their use or the work they do in a sentence. These kinds are called **Parts of speech**.

There are eight Parts of Speech:

A NOUN

A noun is the *name of a person, place, animal or a thing*; as,

(i) *John* is a good *boy*.

(ii) *Delhi* is the *capital* of *India*.

(iii) Her *courage* won her the *honour*.

(iv) *Taj Mahal* is a beautiful *monument*.

Note : The word 'thing' means all objects which we can see, hear, taste, touch or smell.

There is one type of Noun (Abstract Noun) which we can only think of but we can not feel by our senses.

A PRONOUN

A pronoun is a *word which is used in place of a Noun*.

(i) Darcy is a girl. *She* studies in my school.

(ii) John is a cricketer. People like *him*.

In the above sentences 'she' and 'him' are Pronouns because they are used in place of nouns – (Darcy) in the first sentence and (John) in the second sentence.

AN ADJECTIVE

An Adjective is a *word that says more about a noun or a pronoun.*

(i) Dancy is a *clever* girl.

(ii) John is a *nice* boy.

In the above sentences 'clever' and 'nice' are adjectives because they say more about the noun 'girl and boy'

A VERB

A verb is a *doing word*. Through a verb an action is conveyed.

(i) we *saw* a tiger.

(ii) she *wrote* two letters.

(iii) the children *flew* kites.

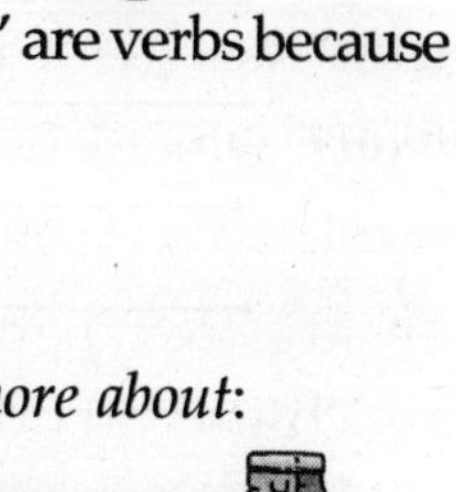

In the above sentences 'saw' 'wrote' and 'flew' are verbs because they convey actions.

AN ADVERB

An adverb is a *word that says something more about:*

(i) *a Verb*

(ii) *an Adjective*

(iii) *another Adverb*

1. She spoke *politely*.
2. This house is *very* beautiful.
3. She spoke *quite* politely.

In the above sentences, the words ***'politely' 'very'*** and ***'quite'*** are ***Adverbs***.

In the first sentence the word ***'politely'*** is ***adverb*** because it tells more about the ***verb 'spoke'***.

In the second sentence, the word ***'very'*** is ***adverb*** because it tells more about the ***adjective 'beautiful'***.

In the third sentence, the word ***'quite'*** is ***adverb*** because it tells more about another ***adverb 'politely'***.

A PREPOSITION

A preposition is a *word which is used with a noun or pronoun to show how the noun or pronoun stands in relation to something else.*

(i) She is fond *of* reading.

(ii) The tired traveller sat *under* the tree.

(iii) There is a spider *on* the wall.

In the above sentences, the words, ***'of'***, ***'under'*** and ***'on'*** are ***prepositions***.

A CONJUNCTION

A conjunction is a *word that is used to join two words, two phrases, two clauses or two sentences.*

Pen *and* pencil

In the above phrase ***'and'*** is a ***conjunction*** because it is joining the words- 'pen' and 'pencil'.

In the office *but* not in the house.

In the above, ***'but'*** is a ***conjunction,*** because it is joining two phrases, 'in the office' and 'not in the house'.

If you work hard *and* if you remain devoted.

In the above ***'and'*** is a ***conjunction*** because it is joining two clauses. 'If you work hard' and 'if you remain devoted'.

I went to market *but* it was closed.

In the above sentence, ***'but'*** is a ***conjunction*** because it is joining two sentences 'I went to market' and 'it was closed.

AN INTERJECTION

An interjection is a word which expresses the sudden feelings of joy, sorrow or surprise.

Hurrah! we have won the match.

Alas! she failed in the entrance test.

In the above sentences ***Hurrah!*** And ***Alas!*** are ***interjections***- the first expressing joy and the second expressing sorrow.

Chapter 7

Kinds of Nouns

Nouns are of four kinds. They are

(i) Common Noun

(ii) Proper Noun

(iii) Collective Noun

(iv) Abstract Noun

A common Noun is a name given in common to every person or thing of the same kind; as,

Darcy is a *girl*.

In the above sentence, the word 'girl' is a common noun because it is a name common to all girls.

A Proper Noun is the name of some particular person or place; as,

Darcy is a clever girl.

London is a city.

In the above sentences 'Darcy' and 'London' are proper Nouns because they are the names of a particular girl and a particular city.

A collective Noun is the name of a number of persons or things taken together and spoken of as one whole; as,

A *herd* of cattle is going.

He was found guilty by the *jury*.

The police fired at the *mob*.

In the above sentences, the words *'herd' 'jury'* and *'mob'* are ***collective nouns***.

An Abstract Noun : is usually the name of a quality, action or state. Abstract Nouns cannot be seen or touched. They are feelings, actions and qualities; as,

Hardwork and *honesty* bring success.

Kindness and *sincerity* are good qualities.

In the above sentences ***'hardwork'***, ***'success'***, ***'kindness'***, ***'sincerity'*** and ***'qualities'*** are ***abstract nouns***.

Chapter 8 The Noun : Number

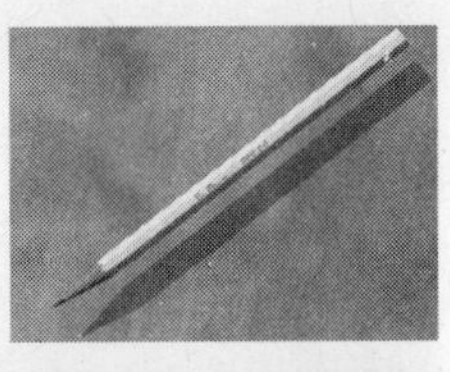

A Noun that *denotes one person or thing is singular Number*; as,

cow, pencil, book, boy.

A Noun that *denotes more than one person or thing is **Plural Number***; as

cows, pencils, books, boys.

Some of the singular and plural Nouns are given below:

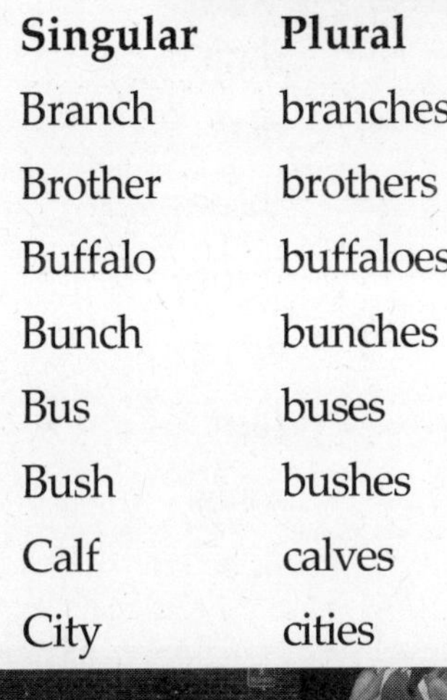

Singular	Plural	Singular	Plural
Actor	actors	Branch	branches
Agendum	agenda	Brother	brothers
Aim	aims	Buffalo	buffaloes
Apple	apples	Bunch	bunches
Army	armies	Bus	buses
Ant	ants	Bush	bushes
Ass	asses	Calf	calves
Aunt	aunts	City	cities
Axis	axes		
baby	babies		
bamboo	bamboos		
Boy	boys		
Book	books		
box	boxes		

Singular	Plural
Child	children
Chief	chiefs
Church	churches
Class-fellow	class-fellows
copy	copies
Commander -in-chief	commanders -in-chief
Cow	cows
Cry	cries
Daughter	daughters
Day	days
Deer	deer
Dish	dishes
Duty	duties
Echo	echoes
Fly	flies
Folio	folios
Foot	feet

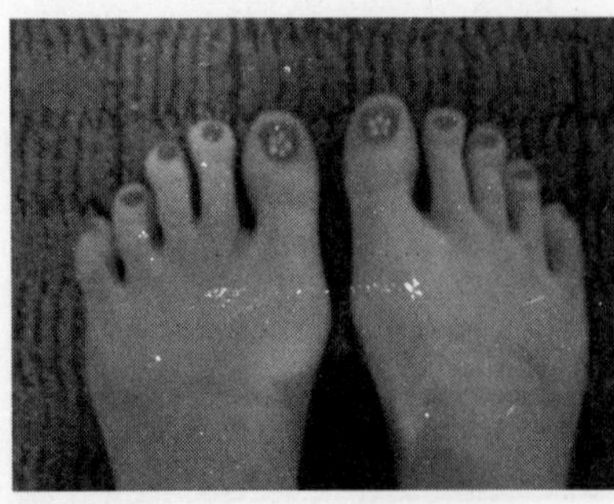

Singular	Plural
Fox	foxes
Gas	gases
Girl	girls
Glass	glasses

Singular	Plural
Goods	goods (always used as plural)
Goose	geese
Gulf	gulfs
Hand	hands
Hero	heroes
Holiday	holidays
Hoof	hoofs
Index	indices
Journey	journeys
Key	keys
Kiss	kisses
Knife	knives

Singular	Plural
Lady	ladies
Leaf	leaves
Life	lives
Louse	lice
Mango	mangoes

Singular	Plural
Maid-servant	Maid-servants
Man	men
Map	maps
Match	matches
Mathematics	mathematics
Memo	memos
Man servant	men-servants
Medium	mediums (media)
Mother -in-law	mothers -in-law
Mosquito	mosquitoes
Monkey	monkeys
Mouse	mice

Singular	Plural
News	news
Ox	oxen
Paisa	paise
Passerby	passersby
Pencil	pencils

Singular	Plural
Pen	pens
Physics	physics
Play	plays
Politics	politics
Puff	puffs
Roof	roofs
Safc	safcs
Scissors	scissors

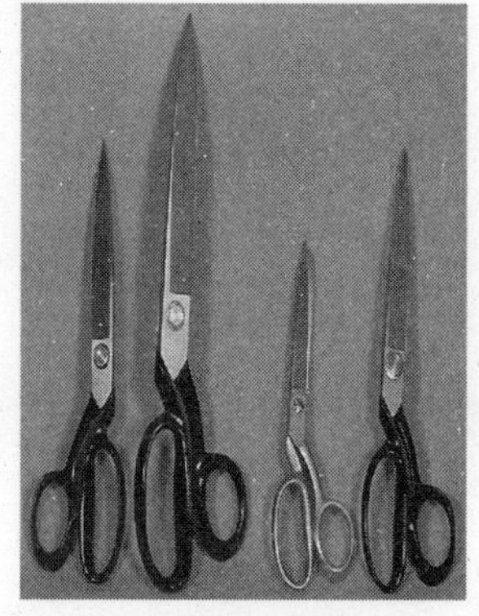

Singular	Plural
Son	sons
Son-in-law	sons-in-law
Star	stars
Stomach	stomachs
Story	stories
Storey	storeys

Singular	Plural
Sheep	sheep

Singular	Plural
Swine	swine
Thief	thieves

Singular	Plural
Tooth	teeth
Toy	toys

Singular	Plural
Trousers	trousers
Valley	valleys
Wages	wages
Witness	witnesses
Watch	watches
Wolf	wolves
Woman	women

Chapter 9

The Noun : Gender

A Noun has four ***genders-Masculine Gender, Feminine Gender, Common Gender*** and ***Neuter Gender***.

A Noun *that denotes a male is called* ***Masculine Gender*** and **a noun** *that denotes a female is called* ***Feminine Gender***.

(All living beings are either of the male or the female sex)

Boy	Girl
Lion	Lioness
Hero	Heroine
Cock-sparrow	Hen-sparrow

The first word of each pair is the name of a *male* animal.

The second word of each pair is the name of a *female* animal.

A Noun that denotes either a male or a female is of the ***Common Gender***, as,

parent, child, thief, person, baby etc.

A noun that denotes a thing which is *neither male nor female* is said to be a ***Neuter Gender***; as,

Pencil, book, house.

Some of the Masculine and Feminine Nouns are given below:

Masculine	**Feminine**
Actor	Actress
Author	authoress
Bachelor	spinster
Bride groom	bride

Masculine	Feminine
Brother	sister
Boy	girl
Bull-calf	cow-calf
Buck	doe
Bull	cow
Cock	hen

Masculine	Feminine
Cock-sparrow	hen-sparrow
Colt	filly
Doctor	lady doctor
Dog	bitch
Drone	bee
Emperor	empress
Father	mother
Fox	vixen
Gentleman	lady
Grand father	grandmother
God	goddess
He-goat	she-goat
Heir	heiress

Masculine	Feminine
Hero	heroine
He-wolf	she-wolf
Host	hostess
Horse	mare
Husband	wife
King	queen
Lad	lass
Lion	lioness
Lord	lady
Land-lord	land-lady
Male-child	female-child
Maternal-uncle	maternal-aunt
Man	woman
Master	mistress
Milk man	milk maid

Masculine	Feminine
Nephew	niece
Peacock	pea-hen
Poet	poetess
Priest	priestess

Masculine	Feminine
Stag	hind
Tailor	tailoress

Masculine	Feminine
Uncle	aunt
Widower	widow
Monk	nun
Papa	mama
Poet	poetess
Prince	princess

Masculine	Feminine
Sir	madam
Son	daughter

Masculine	Feminine
Tiger	tigress

Masculine	Feminine
Washerman	washer-woman
Wizard	witch

Chapter 10

The Noun : Case

When a noun or pronoun is used as the subject of a verb, it is said to be in the *Nominative Case.*

When a Noun or Pronoun is used as the object of a verb, it is said to be in the ***Objective or Accusative Case***.

Note : To find the Nominative, put 'who? Or 'what'? before the verb.

To find the objective or Accusative put *'whom'?* or *'what'* before the *verb and its subject*, as,

(i) He flew a kite

(ii) Dog bit the boy.

In sentence (i) the Pronoun ***'he'*** is the ***subject***. It is the answer to the question ***'who flew a kite"?*** The predicate contains the verb ***'flew'. What did he fly? 'a kite'***. Kite is the object which he flew. The Noun 'kite' is therefore called the object.

In sentence (ii) the Noun ***'dog'*** is the ***subject***. It is the answer to the question-***'who bit the boy'?*** The Noun 'boy' is the object. It is answer to the question –***'whom did the dog bite'?***

A Noun which comes after a preposition is also said to be in the ***Accusative case***; as,

The book is on the table.

Here the noun table is in the Accusative case governed by the preposition 'on'.

Note: The Nouns in English have the same form for the ***Nominative*** and ***Accusative***. The ***Nominative*** generally comes before the Verb and the ***Accusative*** after the verb. They are thus distinguished by the order of words or by the sense.

The ***Possessive case*** of a Noun answers the question ***'whose'?*** as,

This is Johan's book.

Johan's book-the book belonging to Johan. The form of the Noun Johan is changed to Johan's to *show possession or ownership*.

The ***Noun Johan's*** is therefore said to be in the ***Possessive case*** or (***Genitive case***)

Note: The Possessive case does not always denote possession. It is also used to denote kind, 'origin', 'authorship' etc; as,

Dicken's novels	the novels written by Dickens
The Jury's verdict	the verdict given by the jury
Prime Minister's speech	the speech delivered by the Prime Minister
Shiva's temple	the temple dedicated to Lord Shiva.
Birlas' temples	the temples built by Birlas

FORMATION OF THE POSSESSIVE CASE

(i) When the Noun is Singular, the possessive case is formed by adding 's to the Noun; as

The child's toy; the girl's doll

Note: The letter 's is omitted in some words, where too many hissing sounds come together as,

For Jesus sake, for goodness sake;

(ii) When the Noun is plural and ends in 's', the possessive case is formed by adding only an ***apostrophe***; as,

Girls' school,
boys' hostel

(iii) When the Noun is plural but does not end in 's', the possessive is formed by adding 's' as,

Men's hostel, children's notebooks.

(iv) When a Noun as a title consists of several words, the possessive sign is attached only to the last word; as

The Queen of England's coronation.

(v) When the Nouns are in apposition, the possessive sign is put to the latter only; as,

This is Shakespeare, the dramatist's house.

(vi) Each of two or more connected nouns meaning separate possession must take the possessive signs; as

Shakespeare's and Congreve's plays.

USE OF THE POSSESSIVE

The Possessive Case is used with names of living things; as

The Mayor's car

The boy's books

So we may say:

(i) the grill of the window (not the window's grill)

(ii) the page of the book (not the book's page)

However, the Possessive is used in the names of ***Personified objects***, as

Nature's laws

At death's door.

Note: When a non-living thing is treated as a living thing, it is said to be personified.

The Possessive is also used with Nouns denoting 'time', 'space' or 'weights; as,

A week's holidays

In a year's time

A pound's weight

The following use of Possessive is also common:

For mercy's sake.

To my heart's content

At his wit's end

Note: Whenever there is a doubt whether to use a Noun in the Possessive case or with the preposition 'of', 'it is to be remembered that the possessive case is used to denote possession or ownership. Therefore, it is better to say 'the victory of the army' than the 'army's victory'.

DECLENSION OF NOUNS

When various cases of a Noun or (Pronoun) are given in order in the two numbers, we are said to give its Declension. The full Declensions of the nouns 'boy' and 'man' are given below:

	Singular	**Plural**
Nominative Case	boy	boys
Genitive case	boy's	boys'

Accusative case	boy	boys
Nominative case	man	men
Genitive case	man's	men's
Accusative case	man	men

Nominative of Address or the Vocative Case

A Noun used to name a person or thing addressed is in the Vocative case; as,

Johan, come here

In the above sentence, ***Johan*** is the *name of a person spoken to or addressed to*. The following are other examples of ***Nominative of Address***:

(i) come on, girls.

(ii) eat, my child, eat.

(iii) come into my room, Derek.

DATIVE CASE

The Indirect Object of a verb is said to be in the ***Dative Case***; as,

Johan gave a present.

Johan gave Derek a present.

In each of the above sentences, the *Noun 'present' is the object of the verb 'gave'*.

In the second sentence Derek is the person to whom Johan gave a present.

The Noun 'Present' which is an ordinary object, is called the ***Direct object*** and is in the ***Accusative case***.

The ***Indirect Object*** is placed immediately after the verb and before the Direct Object.

Nouns in Apposition

When one Noun follows another to describe it, the noun which follows is said to be in *'Apposition'* to the Noun which comes before it.

Study the following sentence:

Darcy, our English madam, teaches literature.

In the above sentence, 'Darcy' and 'our English madam' are one and the same person.

The Noun 'madam' follows the noun Darcy simply to explain which madam is referred to:

Note: A Noun in Apposition is in the same case as the Noun which it explains.

EXERCISE 9

Separate the Nouns in the following sentences and say whether they are Proper, Common, Collective or Abstract:-

1. The old man walked down to his village.
2. Taj Mahal is situated in Agra.
3. Each soldier was given an award.
4. Health and happiness go together.
5. Honesty is the best policy.
6. He bought a bouquet for my birthday.
7. The crowd threw stones at the policemen.

8. Delhi is the capital of India.
9. A bunch of keys was lost in the bus.
10. Cleanliness is next to godliness.

EXERCISE 10

Write the Feminine Genders of the following Masculine Genders.

1. Lion	2. Cock-sparrow	3. Ox
4. Gander	5. Author	6. Baron
7. Host	8. Count	9. Duke
10. Buck	11. Colt	12. Ram
13. Heir	14. Negro	15. Prince
16. Waiter	17. Peacock	18. Tiger
19. Son	20. Father	

EXERCISE 11

Write the Plurals of the following Nouns:

1. Mango	2. Bird	3. Class
4. Branch	5. Buffalo	6. Potato
7. Woman	8. Foot	9. Maid-servant
10. Son-in-law	11. Knife	12. Story
13. Baby	14. Dish	15. Volcano
16. Cargo	17. Mouse	18. Tooth
19. Child	20. Shelf	21. Step-daughter
22. Commander in-chief		23. Looker on
24. Calf	25. Goose	

Chapter 11 Kinds of Pronouns

Personal Pronouns

I, we, you, he, she, it, they—are called Personal pronouns, because they stand for the three persons', as,

(i) the person speaking

(ii) the person spoken to

(iii) the person spoken of

The Pronouns 'I' and 'we' which denote the person or persons speaking are the ***Personal Pronouns*** of the ***First Person***.

The Pronoun ***'you'*** denotes the person or persons spoken to and is the ***Personal Pronoun of the Second Person***.

The Pronouns *'he'*, *'she'* and *'they'* which denote the person or persons spoken of, are the ***Personal Pronouns*** of the ***Third Person***.

Reflexive Pronouns

When 'self' is added to my, your, her, it and 'selves' to 'our', 'your', 'them', they become Reflexive Pronouns; as.

I enjoyed *myself*.

You enjoyed *yourself*.

She enjoyed *herself*.

He enjoyed *himself*.

We enjoyed *ourselves*.

They enjoyed *themselves*.

In the above sentence *'myself'*, *'yourself'*, *'herself'*, *'himself'*, *'ourselves' and 'themselves'* are **Reflexive Pronouns**.

Emphatic Pronouns

When *'self' and 'selves'* are added for emphasis,, they become ***Emphatic Pronouns***; as,

I *myself* gave him money.

He *himself* said so.

They *themselves* accepted your invitation.

You *yourself* invited him.

Demonstrative Pronouns

These Pronouns are used to point out the objects to which they refer; as,

This is the book he gave me.
Those were only excuses.
That is the fort of Chittorgarh.

Both scooters are in good condition but *this* is better.

In the above sentences *'this'*, *'those'*, *'that'* are ***Demonstrative Pronouns***.

Indefinite Pronouns

All those pronouns which refer to persons or things in a general way, but do not refer to any person or thing in particular, are called ***Indefinite Pronouns; as,***

Somebody has stolen my purse.

Do not harm *others*.

One must do one's duty.

In the above sentences 'somebody', 'others' and 'one' are ***Indefinite Pronouns***.

Relative Pronouns

These Pronouns refer to or relate to some Noun going before; as,

She has returned the book *that* she borrowed.

I have found the book *which* I had lost.

She met Darcy *who* had just returned.

In the above sentences 'that', 'which' 'who' are ***Relative Pronouns***.

Interrogative Pronouns

These pronouns are used to ask questions; as,

Who are you?

Which is the way?

What do you want?

In the above sentence 'who', 'which' and 'what' are ***Interrogative Pronouns***.

Note: Here Pronouns are similar in form to Relative Pronoun, but the work they do is different.

Distributive Pronouns

These pronouns refer to persons or things one at a time. They are always *singular* and are followed by a singular verb; as,

Each of the girls has got a prize.

Either of you can do the work.

Neither of the boys was present.

In the above sentences 'each', 'either' and 'neither' are ***Distributive Pronouns***.

EXERCISE 12

Fill in the blanks with suitable Pronouns:

1. This is the book __________ he gave me.
2. He is the boy __________ stood first in the class.
3. He knew __________ you meant.
4. He is the person __________ we can trust.
5. Teachers like the students __________ work hard.

6. Do you know __________ has happened?
7. No man can lose __________ he never got.
8. He has gone to Delhi __________ is his birth place.
9. This is the instrument __________ they installed.
10. These are the boys __________ have been selected for awards.
11. This is the pen __________ I got as a prize.
12. I saw the snake __________ bit the cow.
13. You cannot have __________ you don't deserve.
14. Darcy got back the money __________ she had lost.
15. This is the gift __________ I have selected for you.

Chapter 12

Kinds of Adjectives

Adjectives may be divided into the following classes:

Adjectives of Quality

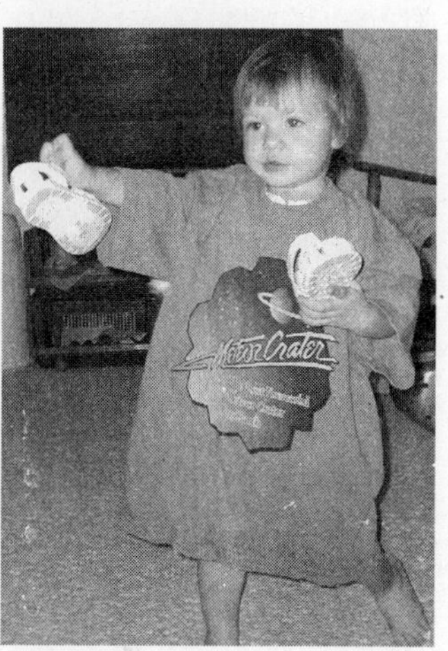

These adjectives show the kind or quality of a person or thing; as,

(i) Johan is a *brave* boy.

(ii) Pamela is a *clever* girl.

(iii) This is a *dark* room.

In the above sentence *'brave', 'clever' and dark'* are ***Adjectives of quality*** as they tell about the quality of Nouns (boy, girl, room).

Adjectives of Quantity

These adjectives show the quantity of a thing; as,

(i) There is *much* sugar in the store.

(ii) She ate *some* rice.

(iii) I gave *sufficient* advice.

In the above sentences *'much', 'some' and 'sufficient'* are ***Adjectives of Quantity***.

Adjectives of Number

These adjectives show how many persons or things are meant; as,

(i) I have *four* books.

(ii) You have committed *many* mistakes.

(iii) He is the *first* boy to enter the class.

In the above sentences *'four', 'many' and 'first'* are ***Adjectives of number***.

Demonstrative Adjectives

These adjectives point out which person or thing is meant; as,

(i) *This* boy is intelligent.

(ii) *That* hill is beautiful.

(iii) *These* books are costly.

In the above sentence *'this', 'that' and 'these'* are ***Demonstrative Adjectives***.

Possessive Adjectives

These adjectives show the possession of a person or a thing; as,

(i) This is *my* house.

(ii) These are *your* books.

(iii) It is *their* house.

In the above sentences *'my', 'your' and 'their'* are **Possessive Adjectives**.

Interrogative Adjectives

'which', 'what' and 'whose' when they are used with Nouns to ask questions, are called ***Interrogative Adjectives***; as,

(i) *what* matter is being discussed?

(ii) *which* book do you like?

(iii) *whose* land is this?

In the above sentences *'what', 'which', 'whose'* are ***Interrogative Adjectives***.

Distributive Adjectives

These adjectives refer to each one of a number; as,

(i) *Each* boy was present.

(ii) *Every* student should bring his own pen.

(iii) *Either* book will do.

(iv) *Neither* blame is true.

In the above sentences *'each', 'every', 'either' and 'neither'* are ***Distributive Adjectives***.

FORMATION OF ADJECTIVES

Many Adjectives are formed from Nouns:-

Noun	Adjective	Noun	Adjective
Boy	boyish	Sense	senseless
Fool	foolish	Silk	silken
Care	careful	Gold	golden
Play	playful	Dirt	dirty
		Storm	stormy
		Pardon	pardonable
		Laugh	laughable
Hope	hopeful		
Trouble	troublesome		
Shame	shameful		

Outrage	outrageous	Man	manly
Courage	courageous	King	kingly
Glory	glorious	Gift	gifted
Envy	envious		

Some Adjectives are formed from Verbs:-

Verb	**Adjective**
Tire	tireless
Talk	talkative
Cease	ceaseless
Move	moveable

Some Adjectives are formed from other Adjectives:-

Adjective	**Adjective**
Tragic	tragical
Whole	wholesome
Three	threefold
Black	blackish
White	whitish
Sick	sickly

COMPARISON OF ADJECTIVES

Adjectives change in form to show comparison—

Positive Degree, Comparative Degree and *Superlative Degree.*

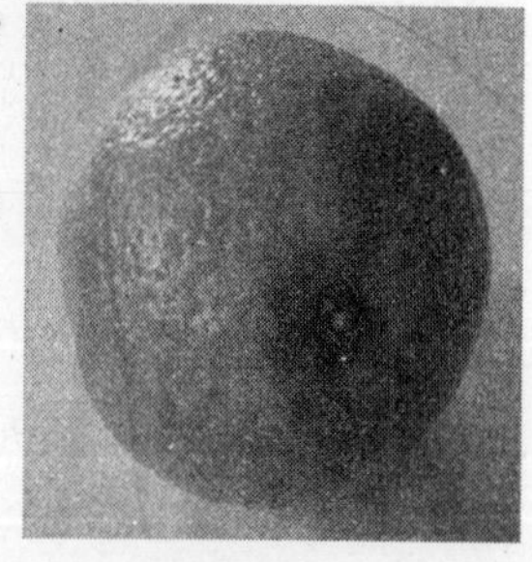

The **Positive degree** of an Adjective is the Adjective in its simple form. It is used when no comparison is made; as,

This orange is sweet.

The **Comparative degree** of Adjective tells about a higher degree of quality than the positive; as,

His orange is sweeter than Johan's.

The **Superlative Degree** of Adjective tells about the highest degree of quality; as,

Your orange is the *sweetest* of all.

Some of the **comparative** and **Superlative Degrees** of Adjectives are given below:

Most Adjectives of one syllable and some of more than one, form the comparative by adding *er* and the superlative by adding *est* to the positive.

Positive	**Comparative**	**Superlative**
Sweet	sweeter	sweetest
Small	smaller	smallest
Tall	taller	tallest
Bold	bolder	boldest
Clever	cleverer	cleverest
Kind	kinder	kindest
Young	younger	youngest
Great	greater	greatest

When the positive ends in *e*, only *r* and *st* are added

Brave	braver	bravest
Fine	finer	finest
White	whiter	whitest
Large	larger	largest
Able	abler	ablest

Noble	nobler	noblest
Wise	wiser	wisest

When the positive ends in *y*, preceded by a consonant, the *y* is changed into *I* before adding *er* and *est*.

Happy	happier	happiest
Easy	easier	easiest
Heavy	heavier	heaviest
Merry	merrier	merriest
Wealthy	wealthier	wealthiest

When the positive is a word of one syllable and ends in a *single* consonant, preceded by a *short* vowel, this consonant is doubled before adding er and est.

Red	redder	reddest
Big	bigger	biggest
Hot	hotter	hottest
Thin	thinner	thinnest
Sad	sadder	saddest
Fat	fatter	fattest

Adjectives of *more than two* syllables, and many of those with two, form the Comparative by using the adverb *more* with the positive and the superlative by using the adverb *most* with the positive.

Positive	Comparative	Superlative
Splendid	more splendid	most splendid
Beautiful	more beautiful	most beautiful
Difficult	more difficult	most difficult
Industrious	more industrious	most industrious

Courageous	more courageous	most courageous
Learned	more learned	most learned
Proper	more proper	most proper

The **Comparative** in *er* is not used when we compare two qualities in the same person or thing.

If we wish to say that courage of Johan is greater than the courage of Derek, we say

Johan is braver than Derek.

But if we wish to say that the courage of Johan is greater than his prudence, we must say.

Johan is *more brave* than *prudent*.

When two objects are compared with each other, the latter term of comparison must exclude the former; as,

Iron is more useful than any *other* metal.

If we say,

Iron is more useful than any metal, that is the same thing as saying Iron is more useful than iron, since iron is itself a metal.

Irregular Comparison

The following Adjectives are compared *irregularly*, that is, their Comparative and Superlative are not formed from Positive.

Positive	**Comparative**	**Superlative**
Good, well	better	best
Bad, evil, ill	worse	worst
Little	less, lesser	least
Much	more	most (quantity)
Many	more	most (number)
Late	later, latter	latest, last

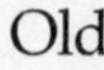

Old	older, elder	oldest, eldest

Far	farther	farthest (distance)
Nigh	nigher	nighest (next)
Fore	former	foremost, first
(In)	inner	inmost, innermost
(Up)	upper	upmost, uppermost
(Out)	outer, utter	utmost, uttermost

EXERCISE 13

Pick out the Adjectives in the following sentences and say to which kind each of them belongs:

1. The storm caused heavy damage to the ship.
2. She is an old and weak woman.
3. There are many errors in your essay.
4. Every man must do his duty.
5. Which book did you select?
6. I have three ball point pens.
7. He died a heroic death.
8. Honest and sincere persons win in the last stage.

EXERCISE 14

Supply a suitable Adjective to each blank in the following sentences:

1. It was a __________ building.
2. I saw a __________ snake in the forest.
3. The __________ prize was won by the Indian.
4. The __________ man lives in a __________ hut.
5. She brought __________ mangoes.
6. I like __________ food.
7. My mother cooks __________ breakfast.
8. The __________ persons seek __________ advice.
9. Sita was a __________ wife.
10. She is the woman of __________ ambition.

EXERCISE 15

Form Adjectives from the following Nouns:-

1.	Happiness	2.	Hope	3.	Heaviness
4.	Sickness	5.	Child	6.	Boy
7.	Woman	8.	Peace	9.	Joy
10.	Quarrel	11.	Friend	12.	Ambition
13.	Sorrow	14.	Laughter	15.	Wonder

EXERCISE 16

Write the comparative and superlative degrees of the following Adjectives:

1.	Brave	2.	Heavy	3.	Beautiful
4.	Ugly	5.	Noisy	6.	Timid
7.	Wise	8.	Noble	9.	Large
10.	Happy	11.	Easy	12.	Hot
13.	Thin	14.	Small	15.	Young

EXERCISE 17

Point out the Adjectives and name the Degree of Comparison in the following sentences:

1. Arthur is a better singer than Daniel
2. She is the best girl of our class.
3. This tea is less hot.
4. He is the idlest boy of our class.
5. The unhappy woman has seen happier days.
6. The Himalayas are the highest mountains in the world.
7. No other country in the world is as hot as Africa.
8. The patient has mild fever.
9. She received the best prize.
10. Your handwriting is untidy.

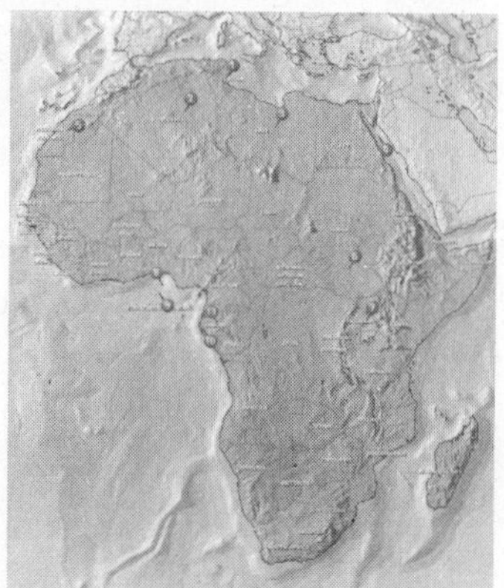

EXERCISE 18

Supply the appropriate Comparative and Superlative Degrees in the following blanks:-

1. Are you feeling ________ today?
2. June is ________ than any other month.
3. Silver is ________ than gold.
4. Common people are the ________ judge.
5. Arthur's work is bad, Daniel's is ________ but yours is the ________.
6. This is the ________ beautiful area.
7. These are the ________ mangoes.
8. You are the ________ friend, I know.
9. My doll is ________ than yours.
10. The Himalayas are the ________ mountains in the world.

Chapter 13 The Action Words (Verbs)

Any action that takes place or happens, is represented by a word called ***'verb'***. You do any work or perform anything, it comes to be known as a verb; also called in other words, the ***'action word'***.

You *run, laugh, jump, talk, work, come or go—— all these are verbs.*

A verb has three main parts: the ***Present, the Past and the Past Participle*** form.

It's good if you remember all the three main parts by heart. Read every verb with all its three parts again and again and remember them by heart. The three forms of some of the verbs are given below:

V_1 **Present form (tense)**	V_2 **Past form (Tense)**	V_3 **Past Participle**
Am, is (be)	was	been
Are	were	been
Arise	arose	arisen
Apply	applied	applied
Awake	awaked/awoke	awaked/awoken
Avail	availed	availed
Bear	bore	borne
Beat	beat	beaten
Become	became	become

Beg	begged	begged

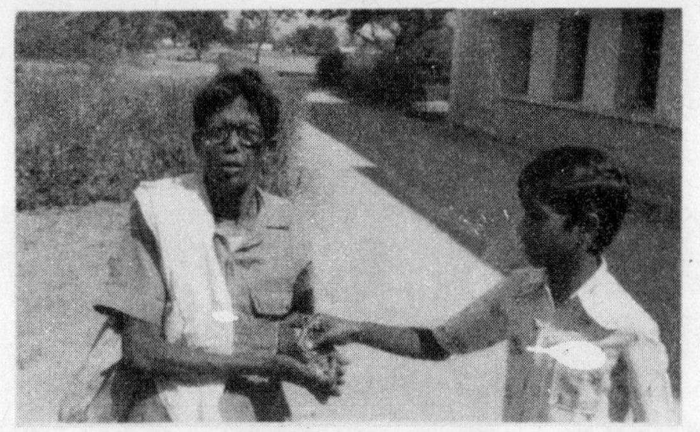

Begin	began	begun
Bend	bent	bent
Bet	bet/betted	bet/betted
Bid	bade	bidden
Bind	bound	bound
Bite	bit	bitten
Bleed	bled	bled
Blow	blew	blown
Break	broke	broken
Bless	blessed	blessed
Borrow	borrowed	borrowed
Bring	brought	brought
Broadcast	broadcast	broadcast
Burn	burned/burnt	burned/burnt
Burst	burst	burst
Bury	buried	buried
Call	called	called
Catch	caught	caught

Carry	carried	carried
Choose	chose	chosen
Clean	cleaned	cleaned
Climb	climbed	climbed

Cling	clung	clung
Come	came	come
Creep	crept	crept
Cost	cost	cost
Cut	cut	cut
Cry	cried	cried
Deal	dealt	dealt
Dig	dug	dug
Dive	dived	dived
Deprive	deprived	deprived
Depart	departed	departed
Differ	differed	differed
Deny	denied	denied
Do	did	done

Delay	delayed	delayed
Draw	drew	drawn

Drag	dragged	dragged
Dream	dreamt	dreamt
Drink	drank	drunk
Decide	decided	decided
Divide	divided	divided
Drive	drove	driven
Dwell	dwclt	dwelt
Dip	dipped	dipped
Drown	drowned	drowned
Eat	ate	eaten
Fail	failed	failed
Fall	fell	fallen
Feed	fed	fed
Feel	felt	felt

Fell	felled	felled
Fight	fought	fought
Find	found	found
Fit	fitted	fitted
Fill	filled	filled
Forbid	forbade	forbidden
Fan	fanned	fanned
Flow	flowed	flowed
Forget	forgot	forgotten
Fly	flew	flown

Fling	flung	flung
Forgive	forgave	forgiven
Free	freed	freed
Follow	followed	followed
Freeze	froze	frozen
Flee	fled	fled
Forsake	forsook	forsaken
Get	got	got
Give	gave	given

Go	went	gone
Grind	ground	ground
Glow	glowed	glowed
Grow	grew	grown
Groan	groaned	groaned
Grumble	grumbled	grumbled
Guide	guided	guided
Gnaw	gnawed	gnawed
Have	had	had
Has	had	had
Hang	hanged/hung	hanged/hung

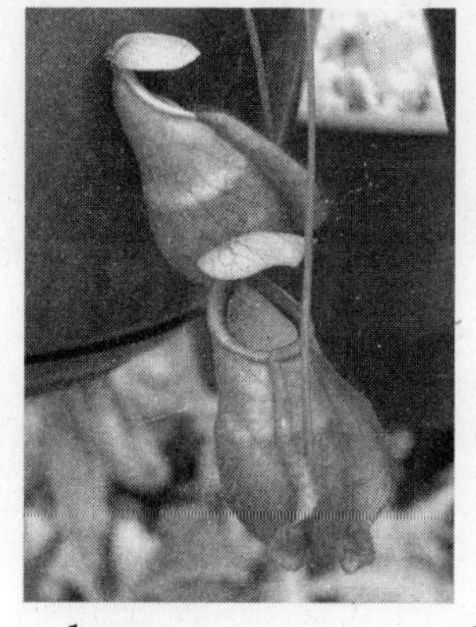

Hung	hung	hung
Hear	heard	heard
Heal	healed	healed
Hide	hid	hid/hidden
Hit	hit	hit
Hold	held	held
Hurt	hurt	hurt

Heave	heaved	heaved
Hint	hinted	hinted
Honour	honoured	honoured
Ignore	ignored	ignored
Illustrate	illustrated	illustrated
Keep	kept	kept
Kneel	knelt	knelt
Knit	knit (knitted)	knit (knitted)

Know	knew	known
Leap	lept	lept
Lay	laid	laid
Lie	lay	lain
Mistake	mistook	mistaken
Meet	met	met
Make	made	made
Mean	meant	meant
Overcome	overcame	overcome
Prize	prized	prized
Prepare	prepared	prepared
Preach	preached	preached

Pay	paid	paid
Rise	rose	risen
Run	ran	run

Ring	rang	rung
Ride	rode	ridden
Sew	sewed	sewn
Shoot	shot	shot
See	saw	seen
Shake	shook	shaken
Shine	shone	shone
Sing	sang	sung
Sit	sat	sat
Slay	slew	slain
Shrink	shrank	shrunk
Speak	spoke	spoken
Smite	smote	smitten
Sling	slung	slung
Sink	sank	sunk
Steal	stole	stolen
Stride	strode	striden

Stick	stuck	stuck
Stand	stood	stood
Strike	struck	struck
Strive	strove	striven
Strew	strewed	strewn
Swim	swam	swum

Sell	sold	sold
Say	said	said
Sleep	slept	slept
Smell	smelt	smelt
Spell	spelt	spelt
Seek	sought	sought
Sweep	swept	swept
Survey	surveyed	surveyed
Spend	spent	spent
Throw	threw	thrown
Tread	trod	trod (trodden)
Tear	tore	torn
Take	took	taken

Tell	told	told
Think	thought	thought
Try	tried	tried
Trace	traced	traced
Thrive	thrived	thrived
Turn	turned	turned
Travel	travelled	travelled
Use	used	used
Understand	understood	understood
Wind	wound	wound
Write	wrote	written

Withdraw	withdrew	withdrawn
Wring	wrung	wrung
Win	won	won
Wear	wore	worn
Wait	waited	waited
Wake	waked/woke	waked/woken
Waver	wavered	wavered

Weap	wept	wept
Beset	beset	beset
Bet	bet	bet
Bid	bid	bid
Broadcast	broadcast	broadcast
Burst	burst	burst
Cast	cast	cast
Cut	cut	cut
Cost	cost	cost
Hurt	hurt	hurt
Hit	hit	hit
Let	let	let
Put	put	put
Read	read	read

Rid	rid	rid
Shut	shut	shut
Split	split	split
Shed	shed	shed
Set	set	set
Spread	spread	spread
Thrust	thrust	thrust

AUXILIARIES

An auxiliary is a ***'helping verb'***, used to make the form of another verb.

The following is the list of auxiliaries:-

be	may, might	ought
have	shall, should	used
do	will, would	need
can, could	must	dare

These are also called ***Anomalous*** or ***Special verbs***. They are the only verbs that come before the subject in questions; as,

Can you swim?

They can combine with *n't* in the negative; as

Isn't, Haven't

Mustn't

The *auxiliaries—can, could, may, might, shall, should, will, would, must, ought, used, dare—* are often distinguished by being referred to as ***Modal Auxiliaries*** or ***Modals***. They express attitudes like permission, possibility, necessity etc.

The *modals can, could, may, might, shall, should, will, would, must and ought* —are ***defective verbs,*** because some parts are wanting in them. They have no—'s' in the third person singular number and they have no infinitive and ***ing*** forms.

Transitive and Intransitive verbs

Transitive Verbs : are those which are incomplete without objects.

Study the following:

(i) She brought

(ii) They killed

(iii) The boys carry

(iv) I made

The verbs in the above — ***brought, killed, carry*** and ***made*** — are ***transitive*** because they do not make sense unless objects are provided to them.

Intransitive Verbs : are those which need not have objects and they make complete sense even without objects.

Study the following:

(i) People laughed.

(ii) The birds fly.

(iii) The old man died.

(iv) The dog barked.

In the above sentence *laughed, fly, died* and *barked*—are intransitive verbs because they give complete meaning even without the objects.

Note: Some verbs can be used both transitively and intransitively; as,

Used Transitively	**Used Intransitively**
The shot sank the ship	The ship sank
Ring the bell	The bell rang
The birds fly	He flies a fighter aeroplane.
The driver stopped the bus	The bus stopped

EXERCISE 19

Write the Past Tense and the Past Participle of the following Verbs:-

Present	Past	Past Participle
Write	________	________
Read	________	________
Speak	________	________
Bathe	________	________
Know	________	________
Tell	________	________
Hear	________	________
Play	________	________
Put	________	________
Feel	________	________
Cut	________	________
Breed	________	________
Shut	________	________
Creep	________	________
Spread	________	________
Lose	________	________
Dance	________	________
Give	________	________
Go	________	________
Come	________	________
Grow	________	________
Hide	________	________

Forget	________	________
Fly	________	________
Flow	________	________
Find	________	________
Get	________	________
Choose	________	________
Begin	________	________
Beat	________	________
Arise	________	________
Bear	________	________
(to bring forth)	________	________
Bear (to carry)	________	________
Kneel	________	________
Win	________	________
Blow	________	________
Become	________	________
Tear	________	________
Sell	________	________
Teach	________	________
Learn	________	________
Buy	________	________
Bring	________	________
Catch	________	________
Seek	________	________
Refuse	________	________
Make	________	________

Telecast	________	________
Broadcast	________	________
Lend	________	________
Quit	________	________
Smell	________	________
Spend	________	________
Think	________	________
Weep	________	________
Burst	________	________
Hurt	________	________
Let	________	________
Meet	________	________
Pay	________	________
Say	________	________
Sing	________	________
See	________	________
Hold	________	________
Ring	________	________
Run	________	________
Shoot	________	________
Shine	________	________
Shake	________	________
Shrink	________	________
Strive	________	________
Take	________	________
Swear	________	________

Throw ________ ________

Swim ________ ________

Wear ________ ________

Build ________ ________

Feed ________ ________

Have ________ ________

Carry ________ ________

EXERCISE 20

Separate the Main Verbs and Auxiliary Verbs in the following sentences:-

1. He met me in the party yesterday.

2. The boys were flying kites.
3. He did not return my money.
4. The girls are dancing.
5. He does not like cricket.
6. You shall be getting a prize.
7. The shopkeepers have downed their shutters.
8. The hounds are chasing the rabbits.
9. The gardener waters the plants everyday.

10. He lost an arm in the battle.

EXERCISE 21

Say whether the verbs in the following sentences are Transitive or Intransitive:-

1. The child is sleeping.
2. He brought a good news.
3. Birds fly very high.
4. The bull struck the man.
5. I know the truth.
6. She read all the newspapers.

7. The tiger roared in the forest.
8. We played tennis.

An Adverb is a word that tells more about:-

(a) a verb (b) an Adjective

(c) Another Adverb

KINDS OF ADVERBS

Adverbs of Time (they show 'when'); as,

(i) He arrived *early*.

(ii) She will come *tomorrow*.

(iii) I *formerly* worked in Indian Air Force.

(iv) She has come here *before*.

In the above sentence—*early, tomorrow, formerly* and *before* are *Adverbs of Time*.

Adverbs of Frequency (they show 'how often')

(i) She has come here *once*.

(ii) They *often* go to temple.

(iii) The accountant came *again*.

(iv) I *always* do my best.

In the above sentence – *once, often, again,* and *always* are *Adverbs of Frequency*.

Adverbs of Place. (they show 'where')

(i) Sit *here*.

(ii) He looked *down*.

(iii) Come *out*.

(iv) I looked *everywhere.*

In the above sentences, *here, down, out* and *everywhere*—are *Adverbs of Place.*

Adverbs of manner (they show *'how'* or *'in what* manner'.

(i) She spoke *politely*.

(ii) He ran *fast*.

(iii) The child crawled *slowly*.

(iv) The student worked *hard*.

In the above sentences—*politely, fast, slowly* and *hard* are ***Adverbs of Manner.***

Adverbs of Degree or Quantity (they show *how much* or *in* what degree).

(i) She is *very* intelligent.

(ii) You were *quite* wrong.

(iii) You are *fully* right.

(iv) The food is *almost* ready.

In the above sentence – *very, quite, fully* and *almost* are ***Adverbs of Degree.***

Adverbs of affirmation or Negation

They show 'yes' or 'no'.

(i) I will *certainly* pass.

(ii) He did *not* know me.

(iii) He *surely* ran fast.

In the above sentence *certainly* and *surely* are the ***Adverbs of Affirmation*** and *not* is ***Adverb of Negation***.

Adverbs of Reason (they show 'the *cause*'.)

(i) I *therefore* left the job.

(ii) He is *hence* eligible to join.

In the above sentence— *'therefore'* and *'hence'* are ***Adverbs of Reason***.

Interrogative Adverbs (they ask questions):

(i) When do you come?

(ii) How did you come?

(iii) Why did you come?

(iv) How do you go to office?

In the above sentences—*when, how, why,* and *how* are ***Interrogative adverbs***.

EXERCISE 22

Identify the Adverbs in the following sentences:

1. She spoke softly.
2. This player runs fast.
3. He often visits this place.
4. You have been badly treated.
5. The boy hit the ball strongly.
6. He slipped and fell down.
7. She is a very intelligent girl.
8. His condition is much worse today.
9. This boy can never steal anything.
10. The soldiers fought bravely.

11. Don't go there.
12. Luckily, everyone escaped unhurt.

EXERCISE 23

Insert suitable Adverbs in the following blanks:

1. I came ________.
2. She closed the door ________.
3. The boys fared ________ in the examination.
4. She sang ________ .
5. Don't go ________ .
6. I can ________ believe it.
7. The girl is ________ shy.
8. He left the house ________ today.
9. I don't decide anything ________ .
10. The principal spoke ________ .
11. You should always aim ________ .
12. We can ________ guess.
13. The patient is ________ better.
14. He ________ comes to our house.
15. The children ran ________ .

Chapter 15

Preposition

Preposition is a word *placed before a noun or a pronoun* to show in which relation the person or thing denoted by it stands in regard to something else.

Study the following sentences:-

(i) There is a flower *in* the garden.

(ii) The child is fond *of* milk.

(iii) The tiger jumped *off* the cage.

In the first sentence, the ***preposition*** *'in'* shows the relationship between two things— *flower* and *garden.*

In the second sentence, the ***preposition*** *'of'* shows the relationship between *fond* and *milk.*

In the third sentence, the ***preposition*** *'off'* shows the relationship between the action expressed by the verb *'jumped'* and *'cage'*.

The meaning of the word ***preposition*** is —*'that which is placed before'*. The Noun or the Pronoun which is used with a preposition is called its ***'object'***.

A Preposition may have two or more objects; as,

The river flows *under* bridge and hill.

In the above sentence, the ***preposition*** *'under'* has two objects—*'bridge'* and *'hill'*.

KINDS OF PREPOSITIONS

Prepositions are of the following classes:

Simple Prepositions

The simple prepositions are—-*at, by, for, with, up, to, till, out, through, on, off, in, from.*

Compound Prepositions

These ***prepositions*** are generally formed by prefixing a preposition to a '*Noun*', an '*Adjective*' or an '*Adverb*'; as,

About, above, across, without, within, along, amidst, among, amongst, around, before, below, behind, beside, beneath, between, beyond, inside, outside, underneath.

Phrase Prepositions

These prepositions are group of words used with the force of a single preposition; as,

In order to	For the sake of	In place of
In lieu of	By way of	In reference to
In front of	By virtue of	In regard to
In favour of	By reason of	In spite of
In course of	By means of	Instead of
In consequence of	By dint of	In the event of
In compliance with	Because of	On account of
In comparison to	Away from	Owing to
In case of	Along with	With a view to
On behalf of	According to	With a reference to
In addition to	With an eye	
In accordance with	With regard to	

EXERCISE 24

Identify Prepositions in the following sentences:

1. She was sitting beside her daughter.

2. The cat is sitting in the corner.
3. The lion and the unicorn fought for the crown.
4. The Piper stopped into the street.
5. They all ran after the dacoit's wife.
6. Such a number of rocks came over his head.
7. The village smith stands under a spreading chestnut tree.
8. He goes to the church on Sundays and sits among his boys.
9. She is fond of architecture.
10. It is natural in every man to wish for distinction.
11. The goat subsists on the coarsest of food.
12. He proved quite a match for the giant.
13. India is teeming with natural wealth.
14. Jaunpur is famous for its perfumes.
15. This tree is associated with scenes of goodwill and rejoicing.

EXERCISE 25

Fill in the blanks with appropriate Prepositions:

1. Do not cry ________ spilt milk.
2. They motored ________ Mumbai ________ Goa.
3. I shall do it ________ pleasure.
4. The river flows ________ the bridge.

5. The dog ran ________ the road.
6. The robber jumped ________ the compound wall.
7. The soldier died ________ his country.
8. The child is afraid ________ the dog.
9. The work was done ________ haste.
10. The property was destroyed ________ fire.
11. She has known me ________ a long time.
12. The moon does not shine ________ its own light.
13. She has not yet recovered ________ illness.
14. We started ________ six ________ the morning.
15. ________ last year I have seen him but once.

Chapter 16

The Conjunction

Conjunction is a *word that joins two words, two phrases, two clauses and two sentences.*

KINDS OF CONJUNCTIONS

Coordinating Conjunction

A coordinating conjunction joins together clauses of equal rank. The chief coordinating conjunctions are — *and, but, for, or, nor, also, either ... or, neither ... nor.*

Subordinating Conjunction

A ***subordinating conjunction*** joins a clause to another clause on which it depends for its complete meaning; as,

(i) I read the story *because* it interested me.

(ii) You should tell him *that* I shall be late.

In the above sentences 'because' and 'that' are Subordinating conjunctions.

The chief ***Subordinating conjunctions*** are— *after, because, if, that, though, although, till, before, unless, as, when, where, while.*

EXERCISE 26

Point out the Conjunctions in the following sentences:

1. He will not succeed unless he works harder.
2. She arrived after you had gone.
3. We waited till the bus arrived.
4. Bread and milk is wholesome food.
5. He will get the prize if he deserves.

6. When you are called, you must come at once.
7. Do not go before mother comes.
8. Since you say so, I must believe it.
9. The soldier fled lest he should be killed.
10. He did not come because you did not call him.
11. He is richer than I (am).
12. I will stay until he returns.

EXERCISE 27

Fill in the blanks with appropriate Conjunctions:

1. Be just__________ fear not.
2. He ran fast, __________ he missed the train.
3. They fled, __________ they were afraid.
4. Make haste, __________ you will be late.
5. I am sure __________ she said so.
6. Wait __________ he returns.
7. You finished first __________ you began late.

8. _________ he was ambitious, I slew him.

9. _________ you eat too much, you will be ill.

10. Arthur is slow _________ sure.

EXERCISE 28

Fill in each blank in the following sentences with an appropriate conjunction:

1. Two _________ two make four.
2. Is her name Darcy _________ Lesley?
3. I shall not go _________ it rains.
4. _________ you run, you will not overtake him.
5. You should not go now _________ it is raining very heavily.
6. You will not get the prize _________ you deserve.
7. She told me _________ you had arrived an hour ago.
8. She is very rich _________ she is not happy.
9. Water _________ oil will not mix.
10. She left _________ we returned.

EXERCISE 29

Join each pair of the following sentences by means of a suitable conjunction. Make such changes as are necessary:

1. My father is well. ______ My mother is ill.
2. He sells bananas. ______ He sells mangoes.
3. I did not succeed. ______ I worked hard.

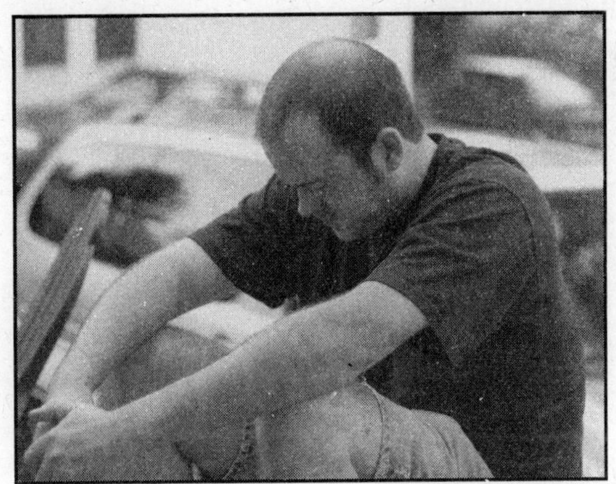

4. We honour him. ______ He is a brave man.
5. He is poor. ______ He is honest.
6. She is rich. ______ She is not happy.
7. I sat down. ______ I was tired.
8. Boys must be quiet. ______ They must leave the room.
9. Arthur did not come. ______ He did not send a letter.
10. It is autumn. ______ The leaves are falling.
11. He lost the prize. ______ He tried his best.
12. You may go. ______ I will stay.

Chapter 17 The Interjection

Interjection is a word that is used *to express some sudden feeling or emotion of joy, sorrow, surprise etc.* Interjections are not related to the other words in a sentences; as,

(i) *Hurrah*! we have won the match.

(ii) *Alas*! she is dead.

(iii) *Hush*! the boss is coming.

(iv) *Bravo*! the spider has climbed the wall.

In the above sentences, *Hurrah, Alas, Hush* and *Bravo* are ***interjections***.

Sometimes, some group of words are also used to express sudden feelings or emotions; as,

Oh God! Well Done! Good Gracious.

Chapter 18

Tense

The word **Tense** comes from the Latin *tempus* which means time:

There are three Main Tenses:-

The **Present Tense**

The **Past Tense**

The **Future Tense**

A verb that refers to the ***Present Time***, is said to be in the ***Present Tense***; as,

(i) I get up early in the morning.

(ii) The sun rises in the east.

A verb that refers to the ***Past time***, is said to be in the ***Past Tense***; as,

(i) I met him in the party yesterday.

(ii) The examination had started when she reached the examination hall.

A verb that refers to the ***Future Time***, is said to be in the ***Future Tense***; as,

(i) I shall play.

(ii) The boys will be singing.

All the three Tenses— Present, Past and Future, have 4 forms each.

PERSONS

Before learning Tenses, it is essential to properly understand 'Persons' which in grammatical terms means ***three classes*** of ***Personal*** Pronouns.

The *person speaking*

The *person spoken to*

The *person spoken of*

Persons:-

1st Person		2nd Person		3rd Person	
I	We	You	you	He She It	They
Singular Number	Plural Number	Singular Number	Plural Number	Singular Number	Plural Number

Simple Present Tense

This tense is used:

To express a habitual action; as,

(i) I get up early in the morning.

(ii) She goes to church on Sundays.

To express general truths; as,

(i) Two and two make four.

(ii) The sun rises in the east.

(iii) Man is mortal.

To indicate a future event; as,

(i) Prime Minister goes to the U.S.A. next month.

(ii) We leave for Mumbai next week.

(iii) When does the school reopen?

Rules : while using this tense, the following rules should be observed:-

(i) Use present form of any Principal verb.

(ii) Use *'s'* or *'es'* with the verb if the subject is third person singular number. (*he, she, it*).

(iii) Use the ***Auxiliary***— *'do'* or *'does'* for making *Negative* and *Interrogative sentences*.

(iv) *'Does'* is only used with *Third Person Singular Number* (*he, she, it*) and *'Do'* is used with all other subjects —(*I, we, you, they*)

(v) When *'does'* has already been used in *Negative* and *Interrogative sentences* 's' or 'es' is not used with the Main Verb.

Example: Following are the examples of ***Simple Present Tense***:

1. I take bath everyday.
2. She takes vegetarian food.
3. My father goes to office at 9 a.m.
4. This magazine appears twice a week.
5. We play cricket on Sundays.
6. Children make a lot of noise here.
7. The sun sets in the west.
8. All men worship God.
9. He runs fast.
10. The judge punishes the accused.

Negative Sentences:

1. I do not take bath everyday.
2. She does not take vegetarian food.
3. My father does not go to office at 9 a.m.
4. This magazine does not appear twice a week.
5. We do not play cricket on Sundays.

Interrogative Sentences:

1. Do children make a lot of noise here?
2. Does the sun set in the west?
3. Do all men worship God?.
4. Does he run fast?
5. Does the judge punish the accused?

Present Continuous Tense

This Tense is used:

To express an action which is going on at the time of speaking as;

(i) The boys are playing.

(ii) I am doing my homework.

(iii) Mother is cooking food.

To express an action that is planned to take place in the near future; as,

(i) I am going to my uncle's house in the evening.

(ii) My wife is arriving tomorrow.

Rules : While using this tense, the following rules should be observed.

(i) The *Auxiliaries*— '*is*' or '*are*' or '*am*' are used.

(ii) '*is*' is used with all *Singular subjects* except *I*.

(iii) '*are*' is used with all *Plural subjects*.

(iv) '*am*' is used with *I*.

Examples : Following are the examples of ***Present Continuous Tense***.

1. I am learning English.
2. My mother is washing clothes.
3. People are watching a cricket match.
4. Birds are singing.
5. Students are writing their answers.
6. Hawker is selling bangles.

Negative Sentences:

1. I am not learning English.
2. My mother is not washing clothes.
3. People are not watching a cricket match.

Interrogative Sentences:

1. Are birds singing?
2. Are students writing their answers?
3. Is hawker selling bangles?

Present Perfect Tense

This tense is used.

To indicate an action just completed; as.

(i) I have just had my breakfast.

(ii) She has left for office.

(iii) The boys have completed their work.

To express those past actions whose time is not definite; as,

(i) I have seen this movie.

(ii) Have you read Mill on the Floss?

(iii) She has already passed this test.

To express an action which began at some time in the past and is continuing up to the present moment; as,

(i) I have so far written him two letters.

(ii) I have known this person for a long time.

Rules : While using this tense, the following rules should be observed:

(i) The ***auxiliaries,*** *'has'* and *'have'* are used

(ii) *'Past Participle'* form of the *verb* is used.

(iii) *'Has'* is used only when the Subject is *Third Person Singular Number (he, she, it)*

(iv) *'Have'* is used with all other *subjects (I, you, we, they)*

Example: Following are the examples of ***Present Perfect Tense***:

1. My father has left for office.
2. The aeroplane has landed.
3. I have read Shakespeare's Hamlet.
4. The doctor has examined the patient.
5. The driver has stopped the train.

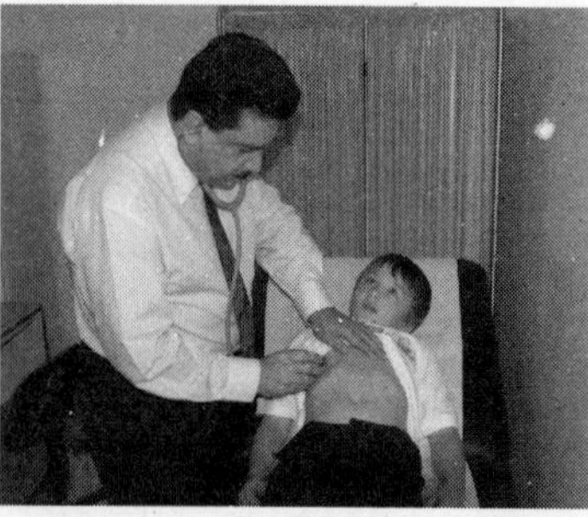

6. You have travelled a long distance.
7. The Municipal Corporation has demolished many unauthorized buildings.
8. She has already seen this movie.

Negative Sentences:

1. My father has not left for office.
2. The aeroplane has not landed.
3. I have not read Shakespeare's Hamlet.
4. The doctor has not examined the patient.

Interrogative Sentences:

1. Has the driver stopped the train?
2. Have you travelled a long distance?
3. Has the Municipal Corporation demolished many unauthorized buildings?
4. Has she already seen this movie?

Present Perfect Continuous Tense

This tense is used :

To denote an action which began in the Past and is still continuing.

Rules : While using this tense, the following rules should be observed :

(i) *'Has been' or 'have been'* is used.

(ii) Present form of the verb + ing is used.

(iii) *'Since'* or *'for'* is used.

(iv) *'Has been'* is used when the subject is *'Third Person Singular Number' (he, she, it).*

(v) *'Have been'* is used with all other *subjects — (I, we, they, you)*

Note : 'Since' is used to denote 'Point of Time' and 'for' is used to denote Period of Time.

Example : Following are the examples of ***Present Perfect Continuous Tense***:-

1. I have been working since morning.
2. The boys have been playing for two hours.
3. The teacher has been teaching the class for forty minutes.
4. They have been watching television since afternoon.
5. They have been living in Delhi since 1974.
6. Radha has been dancing for half an hour.

Negative Sentences:

1. I have not been working since morning.
2. The boys have not been playing for two hours.
3. The teacher has not been teaching the class for forty minutes.

Interrogative Sentences:

1. Have they been watching television since afternoon?
2. Have they been living in Delhi since 1974?
3. Has Radha been dancing for half an hour?

PAST TENSE

Simple Past Tense

This tense is used:

To indicate an action completed in the past; as,

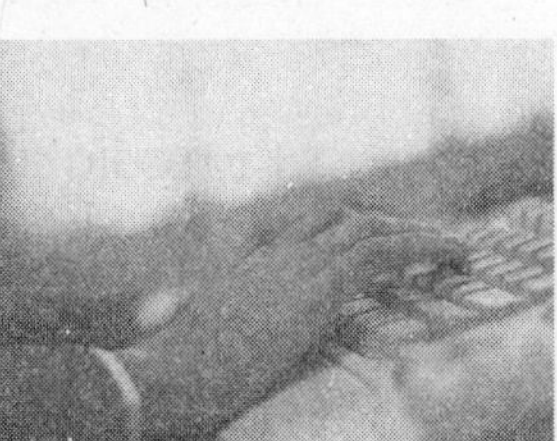

(i) I met him in the party yesterday.

(ii) She wrote two letters last week.

(iii) The typist typed the letters.

To indicate past habits; as,

(i) I went for a long walk everyday. (when I was young)

(ii) She saw a movie everyday.

(iii) We practised maths for hours.

Rules : While using this tense, the following rules should be observed:-

(i) *Past form* of the *verb* is used.

(ii) *Auxiliary 'did'* is used for making *Negative* and *Interrogative sentences.*

(iii) *Present form* of the *verb* is used with *Negative* and *Interrogative sentences* (when did has already been used).

Examples : Following are the examples of ***The Past Simple Tense***.

1. I wrote him a letter yesterday.
2. The Prime Minister gave a long speech on Independence Day.
3. The chief guest distributed the prizes.

4. A film star inaugurated the function.
5. She went abroad last month.
6. India defeated Pakistan in the Kargil War.

Negative Sentences:

1. I did not write him a letter yesterday.
2. The Prime Minister did not give a long speech on Independence Day.
3. The chief guest did not distribute the prizes.

Interrogative Sentences:

1. Did a film star inaugurate the function?
2. Did she go abroad last month?
3. Did India defeat Pakistan in the Kargil War?

Past Continuous Tense

This tense is used.:

To denote an action going on in the past.

(i) The boys were playing.

(ii) I was watching television.

(iii) The girls were singing.

To denote a continuous/persistent habit in the past; as,

(i) He was always disturbing us.

(ii) They were always listening to music.

(iii) The boys were always revising their lessons.

Rules: While using this tense, the following rules should be observed.

(i) The *auxiliary* be (*was/were*) is used

(ii) '*was*' is used with all *singular subjects* and '*were*' with all *plural subjects*.

(iii) *'Present form'* of the *verb* is used.

Examples : Following are the examples of ***Past Continuous Tense***.

1. She was making clay models.
2. I was doing my home work.
3. The girls were dancing.
4. The peasants were ploughing the fields.
5. Mother was cooking food.
6. The maid servant was washing the utensils.

Negative Sentences:

1. She was not making clay models.
2. I was not doing my home work.
3. The girls were not dancing.

Interrogative Sentences:

1. Were the peasants ploughing the fields?
2. Was mother cooking food?
3. Was the maid servant washing the utensils?

Past Perfect Tense

This tense is used:

To describe that action in the past which was completed before another action of the past.

If two actions happened in the past it is essential to show which action happened earlier than the other action. This action is conveyed through a clause of 'Past Perfect' tense and the action which happened later, is put in a clause of Simple Past Tense; as,

(i) I had reached home when rain started.

(ii) She had completed her work when the teacher came.

In the above sentences—-'*I had reached home*' and '*she had completed her work*' are ***Past Perfect*** and —-'*when rain started*' and '*when the teacher came*'— are the clauses of ***Simple Past Tense***.

Note : This tense should not be used unless two actions completed one after the other in the past are to be conveyed in one sentence. To convey a single action of the past, only Simple Past Tense should be used.

Rules:- While using this tense, the following rules should be observed:-

(i) Auxiliary 'had' is used with all the subjects (persons)

(ii) 'Past Participle' form of the verb is used.

(iii) One clause of Simple Past Tense is used to convey the action which happened later.

Examples : Following are the examples of ***Past Perfect Tense:***

1. I had completed the work when my father came.
2. The train had left before we reached the station.
3. The patient had recovered when the doctor came.

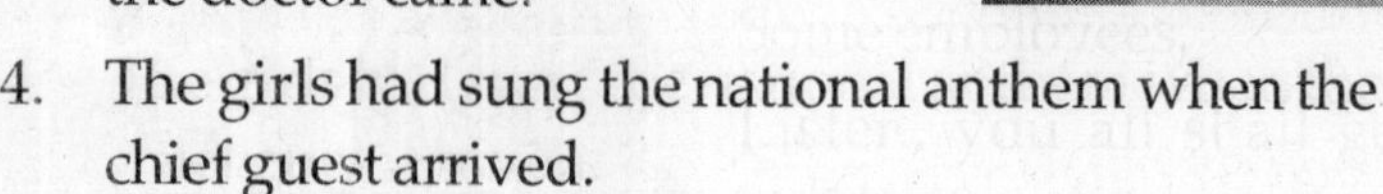

4. The girls had sung the national anthem when the chief guest arrived.
5. She had cooked the food when the guests came.
6. The pilot had baled out before the engine caught fire.

Negative Sentences :

1. I had not completed the work when father came.
2. The train had not left before we reached the station.
3. The patient had not recovered when the doctor came.

Interrogative Sentences:

1. Had the girls sung the national anthem when the chief guest arrived?
2. Had she cooked the food when the guests came?
3. Had the pilot baled out before the engine caught fire?

Past Perfect Continuous Tense

This tense is used:

To denote an action which began before a certain point in the past and continued up to that time; as,

(i) She had been cooking for half an hour.

(ii) The boys had been playing since morning.

(iii) I had been teaching there for nine years.

Rules : While using this tense, the following rules should be observed:-

(i) *'Had been'* is used with all the *subjects*

(ii) *'Present form* of the *verb + ing'* is used.

(ii) *'Since'* or *'for'* is used.

Examples : Following are the examples of the ***Past Perfect Continuous tense:-***

1. I had been studying in Doon Public School since 1995.
2. The labourers had been working since morning.

3. We had been waiting for the bus for a long time.
4. They had been playing football for two hours.
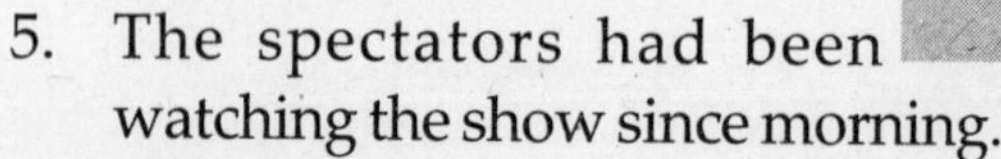
5. The spectators had been watching the show since morning.
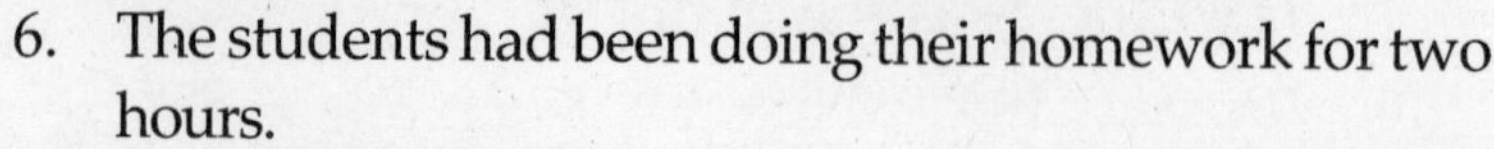
6. The students had been doing their homework for two hours.

Negative Sentences :

1. I had not been studying in Doon Public School since 1995.
2. The labourers had not been working since morning.
3. We had not been waiting for the bus for a long time.

Interrogative Sentences :

1. Had they been playing football for two hours?
2. Had the spectators been watching the show since morning?
3. Had the students been doing their homework for two hours?

FUTURE TENSE

Simple Future Tense

This tense is used:

To describe an action that will take place in future; as,

(i) We shall play a match tomorrow.

(ii) They will return next week.

(iii) We shall go out in the evening.

Rules: While using this tense, the following rules should be observed:-

(i) The *auxiliary 'shall'* or *'will'* is used.

(ii) *'shall'* is used with *First Person Singular Number and Plural Number (I, We).*

(iii) *'Will'* is used with all other *subjects (You, he, she, it, they).*

(iv) *'Present form'* of the *verb* is used.

Note : 'Will' can also be used with *First Person Singular Number* and *Plural Number* but that use is restricted to Modal Auxiliaries.

Examples : Following are the examples of ***Simple Future Tense***:

1. I shall meet you tomorrow.
2. He will come back next month.
3. The Prime Minister will unfurl the National Flag.
4. The hawker will sell his wares.
5. The boys will clean their rooms.
6. The teacher will give a speech.

Negative Sentences :

1. I shall not meet you tomorrow.
2. He will not come back next month.
3. The Prime Minister will not unfurl the National Flag.

Interrogative Sentences :

1. Will the hawker sell his wares?
2. Will the boys clean their rooms?
3. Will the teacher give a speech?

Future Continuous Tense

This tense is used:

To denote an action which will be going on at some time in future; as,

(i) I shall be teaching the class then.

(ii) The boys will be doing their home work.

(iii) We shall be learning our lessons.

To denote future events that are planned; as,

(i) They will be staying with us for one week.

(ii) We shall be participating in the concert.

(iii) He will be joining us next month.

Rules : While using this tense, the following rules should be observed:-

(i) '*shall be*' or '*will be*' is used.

(ii) *Present form* of the *verb + ing* is used.

Examples : Following are the examples of ***Future Continuous Tense***:-

1. Mother will be reading a holy book.
2. I shall be visiting the Taj Mahal next week.
3. The procession will be moving on the main road.
4. The doctor will be examining the patient
5. The Prime Minister will be unfurling the National Flag.
6. The gardener will be watering the plants.

Negative Sentences :

1. Mother will not be reading a holy book.
2. I shall not be visiting the Taj Mahal next week.
3. The procession will not be moving on the main road.

Interrogative Sentences:

1. Will the doctor be examining the patient?
2. Will the Prime Minister be unfurling the National Flag?
3. Will the gardener be watering the plants?

Future Perfect Tense

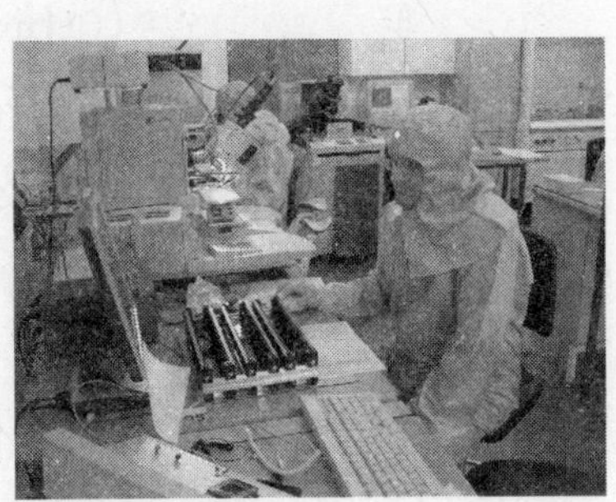

This tense is used:

To describe the completion of an action by a certain time in future; as,

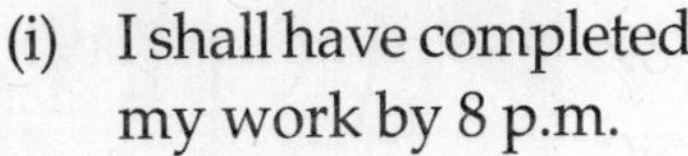

(i) I shall have completed my work by 8 p.m.

(ii) She will have come back by Monday next.

Rules : The following rules should be observed while using this tense:-

(i) *'Shall have'* or *'will have'* is used.

(ii) *'shall have'* is used with *First Person Singular Number* and *Plural Number (I, we)* and *'will have'* is used with all other *subjects, (You, he, she, it, they).*

(iii) *'Past Participle'* form of the verb is used:-

Examples : Following are the examples of ***Future Perfect Tense***.

1. I shall have completed my Board examinations by 2009.

2. She will have completed her painting by evening.
3. The aeroplane will have taken off.
4. The All India Radio will have switched off the transmission by 12 a.m.
5. The guests will have left by tomorrow.
6. They will have dug the earth by then.

Negative Sentences :

1. I shall not have completed my Board examinations by 2009.
2. She will not have completed her painting by evening.
3. The aeroplane will not have taken off.

Interrogative Sentences :

1. Will the All India Radio have switched off the transmission by 12 a.m.
2. Will the guests have left by tomorrow?
3. Will they have dug the earth by then?

Future Perfect Continuous Tense

This tense is used :

To denote that action which will begin in future and will be continuing in future at a particular time; as,

(i) I shall have been studying in Delhi Public School since 2008.

(ii) They will have been preparing for their Board examinations for a long time.

Rules : While using this tense, the following rules should be observed:-

(i) 'Shall have been' or 'will have been' is used.

(ii) 'Shall have been' is used with First Person Singular Number and Plural Number (I, we) and 'Will have been' is used with all other subjects (you, he, she, it, they).

(iii) Present form of the verb + ing ' is used.

(iv) 'Since' or 'for' is used.

Examples : Following are the examples of the ***Future Perfect Continuous Tense***.

1. I shall have been studying for four hours.
2. The boys will have been playing since morning.
3. The driver will have been driving the bus for sixteen hours.
4. They will have been attending the classes since 2009.
5. The spectators will have been watching the match for five hours.
6. He will have been working for us for a long time.

Negative Sentences :

1. I shall not have been studying for four hours.
2. The boys will not have been playing since morning.
3. The driver will not have been driving the bus for sixteen hours.

Interrogative Sentences :

1. Will they have been attending the classes since 2009?

2. Will the spectators have been watching the match for five hours?
3. Will he have been working for us for a long time?

EXERCISE 30

Name the Tense of the following sentences: (Simple Present, Present Continuous, Present Perfect, Present Perfect Continuous)

1. The soldiers have been sleeping for four hours.
2. The sun rises in the east.
3. Students are solving the sums.
4. He exercises everyday.
5. The police have investigated the case.

6. My mother does not speak fluent English.
7. Do you work hard?
8. Are you reading a novel?
9. My mother has been cooking for one?
10. We have been studying in this school for ten years.

EXERCISE 31

Name the tense of the following sentences:-

(Simple Past, Past Continuous, Past Perfect, Past Perfect Continuous)

1. She met me in the party yesterday.
2. Boys were doing their home work.
3. Had you done your home work when the tutor came?

4. The spectators were watching a cricket match.
5. Many students had gone out when the teacher entered the class.
6. Did you return his money?
7. Were they solving the sums?
8. The aeroplane had landed when a very heavy storm blew.
9. I did not meet him in the party yesterday.
10. The Britishers quit India in 1947.

EXERCISE 32

Name the tense of the following sentences :

(Simple Future, Future Continuous, Future Perfect, Future Perfect Continuous)

1. I shall be waiting for you.
2. She will have completed her work by evening.
3. They will start the show at 12 p.m.
4. The peon will ring the bell.
5. Will the boys have been studying since morning?
6. They will not be staying with us.
7. Will you help me?
8. Will you be participating in the concert?
9. They will be attending the class.
10. He will not go to school tomorrow.

EXERCISE 33

Make the followings sentences Negative by making their meaning opposite: ***(Simple Present, Present Continuous, Present Perfect, Present Perfect Continuous)***

1. He comes here regularly.
2. This dog barks very loudly.
3. The sun has set.
4. The boys have been working since morning.
5. I play hockey.
6. He has collected his salary.
7. She speaks softly.
8. They are disturbing us.
9. He cares for the poor.
10. Girls are dancing.

EXERCISE 34

Make the following sentences Interrogative:

(Simple Present, Present Continuous, Present Perfect, Present Perfect Continuous)

1. She knows you.
2. The teacher has finished his lecture.
3. They are solving the sums.
4. I enjoy myself at their place.
5. The child has been crying since morning.
6. The girl is playing with her dolls.
7. The examiner has sealed all the question papers.

8. She speaks fluent English.
9. The hawker is selling bangles.
10. She has been working in this office for ten years.

EXERCISE 35

Make the following sentences Negative (Simple Past, Past Continuous, Past Perfect, Past Perfect Continuous)

1. I wrote her two letters.
2. She had typed all the letters when the managing director came.
3. They spread the rumour.
4. The boys were learning their lessons.
5. This team scored three goals.
6. We had reached the airport when the rain started.
7. Children flew many kites on Independence Day.
8. Girls had been dancing since morning.

EXERCISE 36

Make the following sentences Interrogative (Simple Past, Past Continuous, Past Perfect, Past Perfect Continuous)

1. Farmers sowed the seeds.
2. They had not reached the office when the rain started.
3. The peon rang the bell.
4. They were watching the match.
5. Storm felled many trees.
6. Girls were making clay models.
7. He had been working for six hours.

EXERCISE 37

Make the following sentences Negative (Simple Future, Future Continuous, Future Perfect, Future Perfect Continuous)

1. I shall take rest.
2. He will carry out the work.
3. The tutor will be teaching me tomorrow.
4. He will have been speaking for one hour.
5. I shall have completed my work by evening.
6. The farmers will be ploughing their fields.

EXERCISE 38

Make the following sentences: Interrogative: (Simple Future, Future Continuous, future Perfect, Future Perfect Continuous)

1. They will go for a walk.
2. The pilot will take off at 7 a.m.
3. The farmers will have ploughed their fields.
4. The warriors will fight a duel.
5. Mother will knit a sweater.
6. He will have been studying since morning.
7. The tailor will have stitched your uniform by tomorrow.
8. All the players will receive awards.

EXERCISE 39

Use the correct form of the tense (Verb) given in bracket:

1. I ________ him at the party yesterday. (meet)
2. She ________ English for two years. (learn)
3. He ________ me for a long time. (know)
4. The sun ________ in the east. (rise)
5. She ________ me only two letters up to now. (write)
6. My father ________ ten minutes ago. (leave)
7. This magazine ________ once a week. (appear)
8. My uncle ________ next week. (arrive)
9. I ________ my friend this week. (not meet)
10. Boys ________ their lessons now. (learn)
11. ________ you ________ him? (know)
12. ________ he ________ since morning? (work)
13. We ________ home when the rain started. (reach)
14. The train ________ when we reach the station. (leave) 
15. The children ________ kites on Independence Day. (fly)
16. My father usually ________ home at 9 p.m. but he ________ yet. (come, not come)

EXERCISE 40

Change the following sentences into the corresponding Past Tense :

1. The kite flies in the sky.
2. The girls sing sweetly.
3. Arthur comes of a good family.
4. Birds are singing.
5. My friend writes to me every month.
6. This person swims very well.
7. The teacher punishes the guilty students.
8. I have been waiting for him for a long time.
9. He comes home very late.
10. Girls are making clay models.
11. Darcy knows her work very well.
12. He has been sleeping for a long time.
13. He forgets my name.
14. I go for a morning walk everyday.
15. He makes clay models.

EXERCISE 41

Change the following sentences into the corresponding Present Tense:-

1. He made many mistakes in his essay.
2. He knew me.
3. I wrote to my mother every week.
4. The coward soldier fled from the battlefield.
5. A small stroke felled great oaks.

6. Your gum bled profusely.
7. She cut the vegetables.
8. This child flew many kites.
9. She drank the milk very fast.
10. All people held him in high esteem.
11. He knew his job well.
12. The sun was shining brightly.
13. People were taking a morning walk.
14. She forgot all I told her.
15. It took three days to reach Chennai.

EXERCISE 42

Fill in the Past Tense or Past Participle of the verb given in the following sentences:-

See: I ________ him at the party yesterday.

She ________ this movie last month.

Begin: The movie had ________ when he reached the cinema hall.

The match ________ at 10 a.m.

He ________ to speak nuisance after consuming alcohol.

Run: On seeing the tiger he ________ for his life.

He had ________ five kilometers when we reached the spot.

Tear: In a fit of anger he ________ the letter.

His shirt was ________ .

He is mentally ________ .

Catch: The thief was ________ by the police.

I ________ sight of a new animal in the zoo.

They ________ fish.

Give: The teacher has ________ us a test.

I ________ him a beautiful present on his birthday.

He never ________ them a chance to speak.

Steal: Her purse was ________ by this man.

The burglars ________ money from the almirah.

His heart was ________ by her.

Sow: One must reap what one has ________ .

The farmer ________ the seeds.

Write: He has ________ this essay.

I ________ him a letter yesterday.

Eat: Lunch was ________ in haste.

He ________ his dinner on time.

Say: Who ________ these words?

I have ________ what I wanted to say.

Fly: Where has the bird ________ ?

Many birds ________ in the sky.

Find: Who has ________ my pen?

I have ________ the right answer.

Shoot: Who ________ the tiger?

The poachers ________ down the elephant.

Teach: Who ________ you English last year?

The teacher has already ________ this lesson.

Chapter 19

'Wh' Words

What, whatever, where, wherever, when, whenever, who, whoever, whose, which, whichever, whom etc. are called 'Wh' words.

Out of these, ***what, where, when, who, whose, which, whom*** and even ***how*** are called **Asking Words** or **Questioning Words** as they are mostly used in questions.

Note : '*Who*' is used of **persons**, '*what*' is used for **things** and '**which**' is used both for **things and persons**; as,

Who is that girl?

What do you want?

Which is your bag?

Which person are you talking about?

Where is used for places; as,

Where do you live?

Where is your pen?

Where is your office?

'When' is used for time; as,

When will you come?

When are you going to have your lunch?

When did you return?

When do you plan to go abroad?

How is used for the way or manner something happens or takes place; as,

How did you come here?

How are you?

How will you go back?

How did it happen?

How do you like it?

How did he get out of the building?

'Whatever' means anything or all the things present or available; as,

Whatever you do, do it carefully.

Whatever is left, is enough for us.

One can't get whatever one wishes.

Do whatever you like.

'Wherever' means at any place or at all places (everywhere); as,

You can go wherever you like.

Bring wherever it is.

Wherever you go, come back soon.

He can go wherever he wants to.

'Whoever' means any person or 'all those persons'; as,

Whoever likes it, can take it.

Whoever he is, we don't care.

Whoever wants it, can get it.

'Whichever' means anything out of many; as,

You can take whichever pen you like.

Whichever make it is, it is the best.

You can buy whichever shirt you like.

Whichever pen it is, I want my own.

'Whose' means 'of whom'; as,

Whose books are these?

Whose shirt is this?

Whose pen is that?

Whose stomach is upset?

Whose sister has arrived?

'Whom' means 'the one talked of'; as,

Whom did you ask about her?

Whom are you going to talk to?

Whom does he want?

Whom should I telephone?

Auxiliary is a *'helping verb'* which is used to make the form of another verb.

Apart from 'be', 'have' and 'do', the other Auxiliaries are—***can, could, may, might, shall, should, will, would, must, ought, used, need*** and ***dare***. They are called Modal Auxiliaries or Modals because they perform special functions.

BE

The auxiliary "be" is used:

1. In the formation of the *continuous tenses*; as,

   They *are* playing.

   I *am* studying.

2. In the formation of the *passive voice*; as,

   The shop *was* closed in time.

"Be" followed by the "infinitive" is used:

To indicate a plan, arrangement or agreement; as,

I *am* to meet him tomorrow.

We *are* to be married next week.

To denote command; as,

1. You *are* to solve these sums in ten minutes.
2. Father says you *are* to meet him immediately.

'**Be**' is used in the *past tense* with the perfect infinitive to indicate an arrangement that was made but not carried out; as,

They *were* to have been married last month but had to postpone the marriage until July.

HAVE

The Auxiliary ***have*** is used in the formation of perfect tenses; as,

I *have* worked.

He *has* been working.

'Have' is used with the infinitive to indicate obligation; as,

You *have* to be here before 10 a.m.

He *has* to lift the box himself.

When so used, *have* is either anomalous (i.e. used without *do, does, did* in *negatives* and *questions*) or non-anomalous (i.e. used with *do, does, did*). The anomalous form is preferred when the reference is to a particular occasion. The non-anomalous form is often used with reference to a habitual or permanent state.

Compare the following:

(i) ***Have*** you to get up early tomorrow morning?

(Particular occasion)

Do you ***have*** to get up early?

(i.e. habitually, as a rule)

(ii) I ***haven't*** to go to office today.

I ***don't have*** to go to office on Sunday.

DO

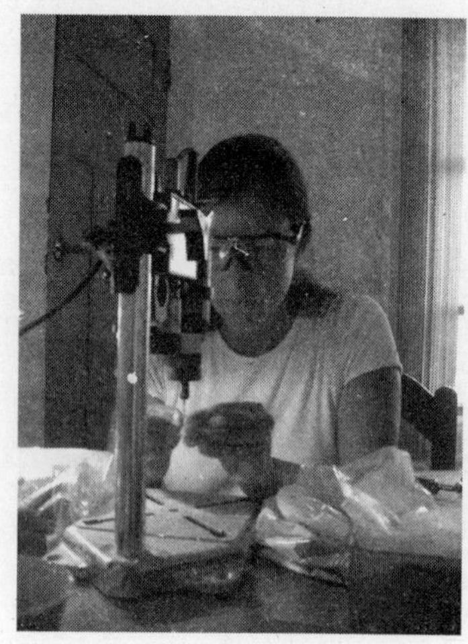

The auxiliary 'do' is used:-

To form the *negative* and *interrogative* of the *Simple Present* and *Simple Past Tenses* of non-anomalous verbs; as,

She *doesn't* work.

She *didn't* work.

Does she work?

Did she work?

To avoid repetition of a previous ordinary (non-anomalous) verb; as,

Do you know him? Yes, I *do*.

He sings well. Yes, he *does*.

You met her, *didn't* you?

He eats mutton and so *do* you.

'Do' is also used to emphasize the affirmative nature of a statement; as,

You *do* look serious.

I told her not to go but she *did* go.

In the Imperative, *do* makes a request or invitation more persuasive; as,

Do be quiet.

Oh, *do* come! It's going to be such fun.

In such cases, *do* is strongly stressed.

Can, could, may, might

Can usually expresses ability or capacity; as,

I *can* swim across the river

He *can* kill a tiger.

Can you lift this box?

'May' is used to express permission. In spoken English 'can' often replaces *'may'*.

You *may/can* go now.

May/can I borrow your camera?

May is used to express possibility in affirmative sentences. *Can* is used in the corresponding interrogative and negative sentences.

It *may* rain tomorrow.

She *may* be at home.

Can this be true?

It *cannot* be true.

Compare the following :

It *can not* be true.

It *may not* be true.

'Cannot' denotes impossibility, while *'may not'* denotes improbability.

In very formal English, _may_ is used to express a wish; as,

May you live happily and long!

May success attend you!

***'Could'* and *'Might'* are used as the past equivalent of _can_ and _may_; as,**

I *could* swim across the river when I was young. (ability)

She said I *might/could* go. (permission)

I thought she *might* be at home. (possibility)

He wondered whether it *could* be true. (possibility)

Note : In present-time contexts *could* and *might* are used as less positive versions of *can* and *may*; as,

I *could* attend the office.

(less positive and more hesitant than I *can* attend the office)

Might/ could I borrow your camera?

A diffident way of saying May/ Can I — — — —?

It *might* rain tomorrow (less positive than it *may* rain)

Could you pass me the salt? (Polite request)

***'Might'* is also used to express a degree of dissatisfaction or reproach; as,**

You *might* pay a little more attention to your appearance.

Shall, should, will, would

'Shall' is used in the first person and 'will' in the second and third persons to express pure future; as,

I *shall* be fifty seven next birthday.

Tomorrow *will* be Monday.

When *shall* we see you again?

You *will* see that I am right.

Note : In present day English, however, there is a growing tendency to use *will* in all persons.

***Shall* is used in the second and third persons to express a command, a promise or threat; as,**

He *shall* not enter my office again. (command)

You shall have a holiday tomorrow (promise)

You *shall* be reprimanded for this (threat)

'Shall' is used in the second and third persons to ask after the will of the person addressed; as,

Shall I close the door? i.e. Do you wish me to clsoe it?

Which book shall I buy? (i.e. what is your suggestion?)

Shall the waiter serve dinner now?

'Will' is used to express

Volition

I *will* - (am willing to) carry your luggage.

I *will* - (promise to) try to do better the next time.

I *will* - (am determined to) succeed or die in the attempt.

In the last example above, *will* is strongly stressed.

Characteristic habit; as

She *will* talk about nothing but music.

He *will* sit for hours browsing the books.

Assumption or Probability; as,

This *will* be the radio you want, I suppose.

That *will* be the peon I think.

Will you? indicates an invitation or a request; as,

Will you have coffee?

Will you lend me your car?

'Should' and 'would' are used as the past equivalents of 'shall' and 'will'; as,

She expected that she *should* (more often: *would*) get a first class.

He said that he *would* be fifty seven next birthday.

She said that she *would* carry my bag.

She *would* sit for hours listening to the wireless (Past habit)

'Should' is used in all persons to express duty or obligation; as,

We *should* obey the rules

You *should* keep your word.

Children *should* obey their parents.

In clauses of condition, *should* is used to express a supposition that may not be true.

If it *should* rain, we shall not go.

If he *should* see me here, he will be annoyed.

'Should' and 'would' are also used as in the examples below:

(i) I *should* like you to help him.

'*Should/ would* like' is a polite form of '*want*'.

(ii) *Would* you lend me your car please?

'*Would* you'? is more polite than *will* you?

(iii) You *Should* have been more careful (*should* + perfect infinitive indicates a past obligation that was not fulfilled.)

(iv) She *should* be in the auditorium now (Expresses probability)

I wish you *would* deliver the message personally (*would* after *wish* expresses a strong desire).

Must, Ought

Must expresses

Necessity or obligation; as,

All *must* obey the rules.

We *must* work or starve.

Fixed determination; as,

I *must* have my way in this matter.

He *must* be fifty now.

Ought (to) expresses moral obligation or desirability; as,

We *ought* to love our neighbours.

We *ought* to help the poor.

We *ought* to know better.

Ought may also express strong probability; as,

Sabrina *ought* to win.

The movie *ought* to be a great success.

Used (to) Need, Dare

The auxiliary *used (to)* expresses a discontinued habit; as,

I *used to* walk a lot when I was young

There *used* to be a cinema hall here.

Note : Used (to) is an anomalous verb. In colloquial English, however, 'Did you use to' and 'did not use to' usually replace 'used to' and 'used not to'.

The auxiliary ***need,*** denoting necessity or obligation, can be conjugated with or without ***do***. When conjugated with ***do***, it has no *–s* or *–ed* forms and is used with an infinitive without *to* only in *negative* and *interrogative sentences* and in sentences that contain *semi-negative words* like '*scarcely*' and '*hardly*'.

You *need* not go (It is not necessary for you to go)

Need I send him a message?

I *need* hardly take your help.

When conjugated with *do,* need has the usual forms— ***needs, needed*** and is used with a *to*-infinitive. It is commonly used in negatives and questions; it sometimes occurs in affirmative also.

Does he need to go now?

I *don't* need to meet her.

One *needs* to be cautious.

Compare the following :

(i) You didn't need to buy it. (= It was not necessary for you to buy it and you didn't buy it).

(ii) I needn't have bought it. (= It was not necessary for me to buy it, but I bought it).

The auxiliary ***dare*** (= be brave enough to), as distinct from the ordinary verb dare (challenge), does not take—*s* in the *third person singular Number* (***present tense***).

It is generally used in negative and interrogative sentences. When conjugated without *do,* it is followed by an infinitive without *to*: when conjugated with *do,* it takes an infinitive with or without *to,* after it.

He *dare* not enter my house.

How *dare* you disobey me?

She *dared* not do it.

She *doesn't* dare speak to me.

EXERCISE 43

Choose the correct alternative in the following sentences:-

1. I don't think I (shall, should, can) be able to go.
2. She (shall, will, dare) not pay unless compelled.
3. You (should, would, ought) be punctual.
4. I wish you (should, would, must) tell me earlier.
5. (Shall, will, would) I assist you?
6. (Shall, should, would) you please help me with this?
7. One (ought, should, must) to pay one's debts.
8. He said I (can, might, should) use his mobile phone any time.
9. If you (shall, should, would) see her, give her my regards.
10. She (need, dare, would) not ask for a raise for fear of losing her job.
11. I (needn't to see, needn't have seen, didn't need to see) her, so I sent a letter.
12. (Shall, might, could) you show me the way to the station?
13. To save his life, he ran fast, and (would, could, was able to) reach safely.
14. She (would, used, ought) to be an atheist but she believes in God.
15. You (needn't, mustn't, won't) light a match, the room is full of gas.

16. The Lok Sabha Speaker (would, need, is to) make a statement tomorrow.
17. She (couldn't wait, didn't need to wait', needn't have waited) for me; I could have found the way all right.
18. I was afraid that if I asked him again he (can, may, might) refuse.
19. He (shall, will, dare) sit outside his garden gate for hours at a time, looking at the passing traffic.

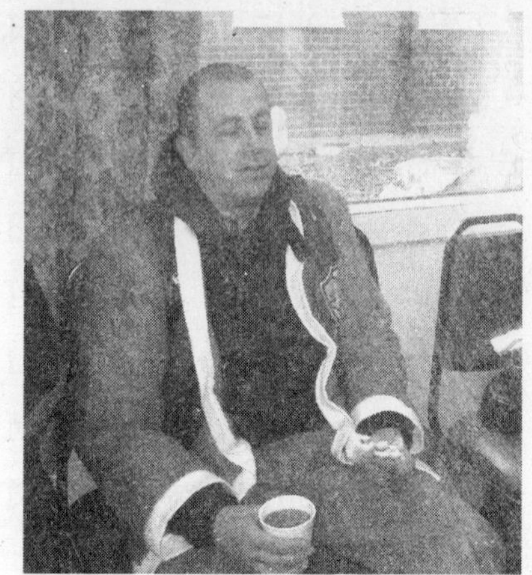

20. (Should, would, shall) you like another cup of tea?
21. I wish he (should, would, will) not play his music system so loudly.
22. I (am to leave, would leave, was to have left) on Friday but on Friday I had a high fever, so I decided to wait till Sunday.
23. I (used, am used, was used) to play cricket when I was in Indian Air Force.
24. (shall, will, would) I carry the suitcase into the house for you?
25. She (will, can, might) come, but I should be surprised.

IS/ AM/ ARE

A. Is the child weeping?
B. Yes, he is./ No, he isn't.

A. Are you going to college now?
B. Yes, I am./ No, I'm not.

A. Is somebody knocking at the door?
B. Nobody is knocking at the door.

A. Are they playing football?
B. Yes, they are./ No, they aren't. No, they are playing hockey.

A. Are you speaking the truth?
B. Yes, I am./ No, I'm not.

A. Are you writing a letter?
B. Yes, I am./ No, I'm not.

A. Am I disturbing you?
B. Yes, you are./ No, you aren't.

A. Am I speaking to Mr. Daniel?
B. Yes, you are./ No, you aren't.

A. Is Johan waiting for me?
B. Yes, he is./ No, he isn't.

DO, DOES:-

Johan : Do you know me?
Darcy : Yes I do./ No I don't.

Johan : Do you like to go for a morning walk?
Darcy : Yes, I do./ No, I don't.

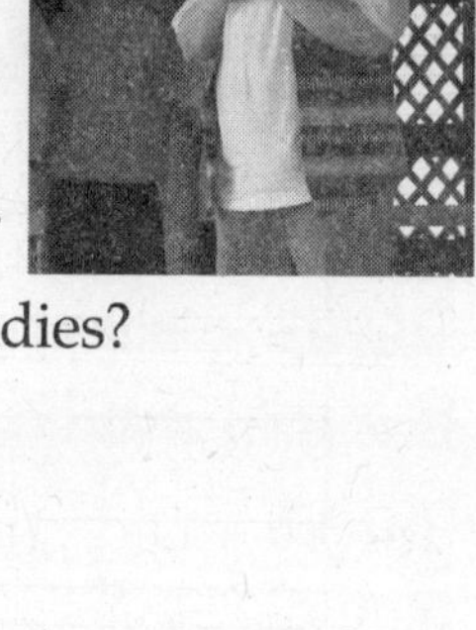

John : Does Joseph sing well?
Darcy : Yes, he does./ No, he doesn't.

Johan : Do you stay in London?
Darcy : Yes, I do./ No, I stay in Scotland.

Johan : Do these boys take interest in studies?
Darcy : Yes, they do./ No, they don't.

Johan : Does Jeoffery swim well?
Darcy : Yes, he does./ No, he doesn't.

Johan : Do you know how to drive a car?
Darcy : Yes, I do./ No, I don't.

HAS, HAVE

A. Have you seen this movie?
B. Yes, I have./ No, I haven't.

A. Has Darcy gone to college?
B. Yes, she has./ No, she hasn't.

A. Have you had your lunch?
B. Yes, I have./ No, I haven't.

A. Has your father came back from the tour?
B. Yes, he has./ No, he hasn't.

A. Have you completed your home work?
B. Yes, I have. /No, I haven't.

A. Have the students taken their tests?
B. Yes, they have./ No, they haven't.

A. Has Johan returned your money?
B. Yes, he has./ No, he hasn't.

A. Have the boys gone on trekking?
B. Yes, they have./ No, they haven't.

DID

Mujib : Did you give him the message?
Ismail : Yes, I did./ No, I didn't./ Sorry, I forgot.

Mujib : Did you get up late?
Ismail : Yes, I did./ No, I didn't./ No, I got up early.

Mujib : Did you see Aftab in the party yesterday?
Ismail : Yes, I did./ No, I didn't.

Mujib : Did you go on a historical visit?
Ismail : Yes, I did./ No, I didn't.

Mujib : Did he visit you yesterday?
Ismail : Yes, he did./ No, he didn't./ No, he visited me today.

Mujib : Did you visit the book fair?
Ismail : Yes, I did./ No, I didn't.

Mujib : Did you help the poor boy?
Ismail : Yes, I did./ No, I didn't.

Mujib : Did Maqbool attend the meeting?
Ismail : Yes, he did./ No, he didn't.

Mujib : Did you like his painting?
Ismail : Yes, I did./ No, I didn't.

Mujib : Did the boys disturb you?
Ismail : Yes, they did./ No, they didn't.

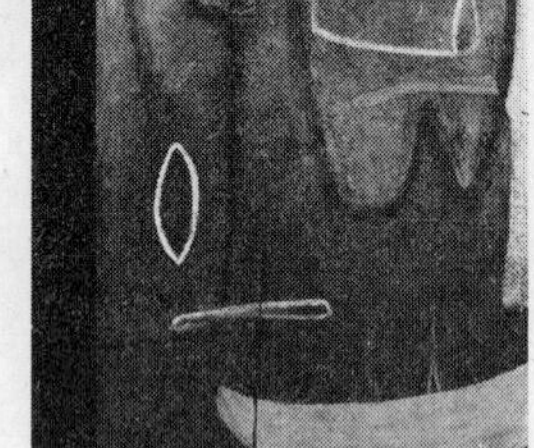

WAS, WERE

A. Were you watching a cricket match?
B. Yes, I was./ No, I wasn't.

A. Was she making a noise?
B. Yes, she was./ No she wasn't.

A. Were they disturbing you?
B. Yes, they were./ No, they weren't.

A. Was she making clay models?
B. Yes, she was./ No, she wasn't.

A. Were you doing your home work?
B. Yes, I was./No, I wasn't.

A. Were the girls dancing?
B. Yes, they were./ No, they weren't.

A. Was the child crying?
B. Yes, he was./ No, he wasn't.

A. Were the students solving their sums?
B. Yes, they were./ No, they weren't.

A. Was the doctor examining the patient?
B. Yes, he was./ No, he wasn't.

A. Was mother cooking food?
B. Yes, she was./ No, she wasn't.

A. Was the girl knitting a sweater?
B. Yes, she was./ No, she wasn't.

A. Was the maid washing the utensils?
B. Yes, she was./ No, she wasn't.

A. Were they sweeping the floor?
B. Yes, they were./ No, they weren't.

HAD

A. Had you completed the work when your father came?
B. Yes, I had./ No, I hadn't.

A. Had the boys solved the sums when the teacher entered the class room?
B. Yes, they had./ No, they hadn't.

A. Had the train left before you reached the platform?
B. Yes, it had./ No, it hadn't.

A. Had the aeroplane taken off when you reached the air port?
B. Yes, it had./ No, it hadn't.

A. Had the girls sung the national anthem before the chief guest arrived?
B. Yes, they had./ No, they hadn't.

A. Had you cooked the food when the guests came?
B. Yes, I had./ No, I hadn't.

A. Had the pilot baled out before the engine caught fire?
B. Yes, he had./No, he hadn't.

HAD BEEN

A. Had you been studying in Doon Public School since 2003?
B. Yes, I had been/ No, I hadn't been.

A. Had the labourers been working since morning?
B. Yes, they had been/ No, they hadn't been.

A. Had the students been learning their lessons for a long time?
B. Yes, they had been./ No, they hadn't been.

A. Had you been waiting for the bus for one hour?
B. Yes, I had been/ No, I hadn't been.

A. Had the cook been cooking since morning?
B. Yes, he had been./ No, he hadn't been.

A. Had the spectators been watching the cricket match since morning?
B. Yes, they had been./ No, they hadn't been.

A. Had you been learning guitar for a long time?
B. Yes, I had been./ No, I hadn't been.

SHALL/ WILL

A. Will you meet him tomorrow?
B. Yes, I shall./ No, I shan't.

A. Will he come back next month?
B. Yes, he will./ No he won't.

A. Will you have lunch in a restaurant?
B. Yes, we shall./No we shan't.

A. Will the Prime Minister unfurl the National Flag?
B. Yes, he will./No, he won't.

A. Will he obey his parents?
B. Yes, he will./No, he won't.

A. Will you help us in our difficulty?
B. Yes, we shall./No, we shan't.

A. Will mother bring milk?
B. Yes, she will./No, she won't.

A. Will you lend me your camera?
B. Yes, I shall./No, I shan't.

A. Will the teacher give your report card?
B. Yes, he will./No, he won't.

SHALL BE/ WILL BE

A. Will you be sleeping then?
B. Yes, I shall be./ No, I shan't be.
A. Will the boys be doing their home work?
B. Yes, they will be./ No, they won't be.
A. Will father be reading the newspaper?
B. Yes, he will be./ No, he won't be.
A. Will mother be cooking food?
B. Yes, she will be./ No, she won't be.

A. Will they be staying with you for two weeks?
B. Yes, they will be./ No, they won't be.

A. Will the gardener be watering the plants?
B. Yes, he will be./ No, he won't be.

A. Will you be watching T.V.?
B. Yes, I shall be./ No, I shan't be.

A. Will the girls be doing rehearsal for the function?
B. Yes, they will be./ No, they won't be.

A. Will you be visiting the Taj Mahal next week?
B. Yes, I shall be./ No, I shan't be.

SHALL HAVE/ WILL HAVE

A. Will you have completed your Board examination by 2008?
B. Yes, I shall have./ No, I shan't have.

A. Will the boys have decorated the room?
B. Yes, they will have./ No, they won't have.

A. Will the train have left the platform before we reach there?
B. Yes, it will have./ No, it won't have.

A. Will she have completed her painting by evening?
B. Yes, she will have./ No, she won't have.

A. Will the aeroplane have taken off before sunset?
B. Yes, it will have./ No, it won't have.

A. Will you have completed your home work by evening?
B. Yes, I shall have./ No, I shan't have.

A. Will the guests have left by tomorrow?
B. Yes, they will have./ No, they won't have.

A. Will you have taken your lunch by 2 p.m?
B. Yes, I shall have./ No, I shan't have.

SHALL HAVE BEEN/WILL HAVE BEEN

A. Will the doctors have been examining the patients for a long time?
B. Yes, they will have been./ No, they won't have been.

A. Will you have been working in this company for six years?
B. Yes, I shall have been./ No, I shan't have been.

A. Will the girls have been singing for one hour?
B. Yes, they will have been./ No, they won't have been.

A. Will they have been working for intelligence service for a long time?
B. Yes, they will have been./ No, they won't have been.

A. Will your parents have been staying in Delhi since 2002?
B. Yes, they will have been./ No, they won't have been.

HOW MANY, HOW MUCH, HOW FAR

A. How many sisters are you?

B. We are three sisters.

A. How many flowers are there in the flower pot?
B. There are many flowers in the flower pot.

A. How many persons are there in the bus?
B. There are thirty five persons in the bus.

A. How many stars are there in the sky?
B. There are a few stars in the sky.

A. How many bananas were there in the basket?
B. There were many/a few/a lot of/ bananas in the basket.

A. How many monkeys were there in the zoo?
B. There were a lot of/ many/ a few/ monkeys in the zoo.

A. How much rice is there in the godown?
B. There is a lot of/a little rice in the godown.

A. How much water is there in the vessel?
B. There is a lot of/ a little water in the vessel.

A. How much ink is there in the inkpot?
B. There is a lot of/ a little/ ink in the inkpot.

A. How much money is left in the house?
B. There is a lot of/ a little/ money left in the house.

A. How far is your home from this place?
B. It is ten kilometres from this place.

WH- WORDS AND HOW

A. What is your name?
B. My name is Johan.

A. In which block do you live?
B. I live in block No. 38.

A. What is your father?
B. My father is an engineer.

A. How old are you?
B. I am thirty six years old.

A. What is the name of your school?
B. The name of my school is St. Anthony Senior Secondary School.

A. In which class do you study?
B. I study in tenth class.

A. How far is your school from your house?
B. My school is ten kilometres from my house.

A. How do you go to your school?
B. I go to my school by bus.

A. Which subject do you like the most?
B. I like History the most.

A. Which type of books do you like?
B. I like story books.

A. Which English dramatist do you like the most?
B. I like Shakespeare the most.

A. How many books are there in your library?
B. There are about three thousand books in my library.

A. When do you go to School?
B. I go to school at 8 a.m.

A. Where do you live?
B. I live in Church Street, London.

CAN, COULD, MAY, MIGHT

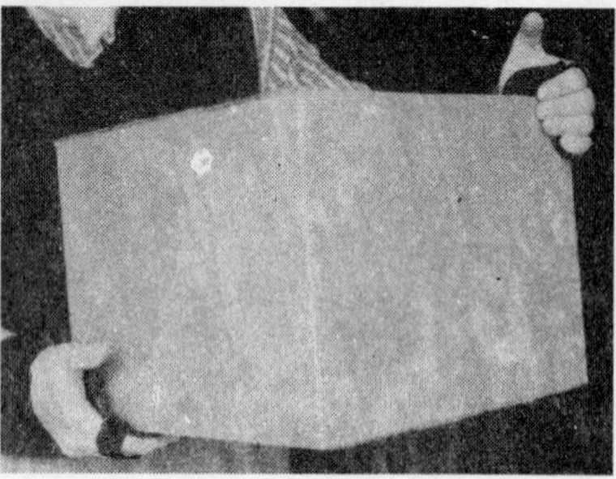

A. Can you lift this box?
B. Yes, I can.

A. Can I beat him?
B. No, you can't.

A. Can I speak?
B. Yes, you can.

A. Can I make a guess?
B. Yes, you can.

A. Can I play in the room?
B. No, you can't.

A. Can you see the blackboard?
B. Yes, we can.

A. Can you solve this sum?
B. Yes, I can/ No, I can't.

A. Can you swim across the river?
B. Yes, I can/ No, I can't.

A. Can he work this sum?
B. Yes, he can/No, he can't.

A. May I come in?
B. Yes, you may.

A. May/ Can I borrow your bicycle?
B. Yes, you may/can/No, you may not/ You can't.

A. Might/Could I borrow your bicycle?
B. Yes, you might/could/No, you might not/couldn't.

A. Could you pass me the salt?
B. Yes, I could/Oh, sure.

SHALL, SHOULD, WILL, WOULD

A. When shall we see you again?
B. You can see me any day next week.

A. Shall I open the door?
B. Yes, you can.

A. Will you carry my books?
B. Oh sure/ It is my pleasure.

A. Should I help him?
B. Yes, you should./ No, you shouldn't.

A. Will you lend me your scooter?
B. Oh, sure/ It is my pleasure.

MUST, OUGHT

A. Must I obey Mr. X?
B. Yes, you must.

A. Ought we to love our neighbours?
B. Yes, you ought to.

Chapter 22

Conversation

(1)

Arthur : Hello! Could I speak to Mr. Johan?

Mrs. Johan : May I know who is on the line?

Arthur : I am Arthur.

Mrs. Johan : Good morning Mr. Arthur, I am Mrs. Johan.

Arthur : Very good morning Mrs. Johan, How are you Mrs. Johan?

Mrs. Johan : I am fine, thank you.

Arthur : Is Mr. Johan not at home?

Mrs. Johan : Sorry, Mr. Arthur. He is not. You can leave message for him.

Arthur : Please ask him to ring me up.

Mrs. Johan : Fine.

Arthur : Thank you, Mrs. Johan.

(2)

Hi Mathews! How are you?

I am fine. What about you?

I am also fine.

I am surprised to see you here.

Yes, I have just come to visit your place.

Oh, so nice of you. Let's go in.

Oh, sure.

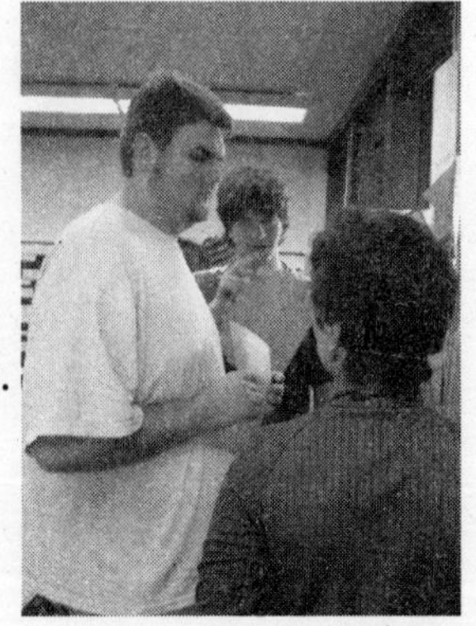

(3)

Robin : Good morning, Miss Darcy. How are you?

Darcy : I'm fine. Thank you. How are you Mr. Robin?

Robin : I am fine, thank you.

Robin : Miss Darcy, this is Miss Mary.

Mary : How do you do Miss Darcy?

Darcy : How do you do Miss Mary?

(4)

A : Where are you going?

B : I am going to watch the cricket match.

A : Let me come with you.

B : Well, come on.

(5)

A. Where do you live?
B. I live in Bharatpur.

A. How far is it from here?
B. It is about eight kilometers.

A. Is it a village?
B. No, it is a big town.

A. What is your business there?
B. I have a medical store.

A. How is your business going on?
B. It is running well.

(6)

Do you know me?

Sorry, I don't (Don't say I don't know you)

But I do?

How? Please.

Do you remember your bus journey on 3rd August?

Oh, yes! Ms. Darcy.

Exactly.

(7)

Do you recognize me?

Yes, I do.

Tell me who am I?

You are Mr. Arthur.

That is right. You have a sharp memory.

(8)

Where are the tables?
They are in the room.
They are old tables.
Where is the calendar?
It is on the wall.
It is a small calendar.

(9)

Do you read the Hindustan Times?

Yes, I do.

Is it a good newspaper?

Yes, it's simply wonderful. I read it regularly.

(10)

Please get me a number—2726890.

Kindly hold on.

(After a few seconds)

The number is engaged sir. May I try it again after sometime?

Please do.

(11)

Do you hear something?

No, I don't.

But I do.

Sorry, I don't.

(12)

May I come in sir?

Yes please, are you Mr. Robert?

Yes, sir.

Please take a seat.

Thank you.

What can I do for you?

I have come to collect money for the repairs done.

All right. Here is your cheque.

Thank you.

You are most welcome.

(13)

What is your name?
My name is Bruce.
How old are you?
I'm eighteen years old.
Darcy is my cousin.
What colour are her eyes?
They are black.
What colour is her hair?
It's blonde.
Is she short?
No, she is tall.
Where are you from?
I am from London.

(14)

Ms. Hoover is teaching English.
She is standing.
The students are listening.
They are learning English.
I am writing in the note-book.
You are looking at the teacher.

(15)

We are sitting.
Arthur is asking a question.
The teacher is answering.
The students are learning English.

(15A)

Mr. Brown is the teacher.

What is he teaching?

He is teaching English.

Where are the teacher's books?

They are on the desk.

That is Johanson?

What is he doing?

He is learning English.

(16)

A. Sir, what can I do for you?

B. I want to get my bicycle repaired.

A. What is wrong with it?

B. Its chain comes off again and again. Pedals produce an irritating sound and the mudguards are not in proper condition.

A. O.K. sir, it will take at least two hours to repair it.

B. I shall come back after two hours.

(17)

A. Excuse me, sir. Could you tell me the way to the bus stop?

B. Yes, please walk about forty metres straight and then take first left turn at the red light. You will get to the bus stop.

A. Thank you.

B. You are welcome.

(18)

Do you see movies?

Yes, I very much do.

What type of movies do you like?

Action movies. I love them.

Latin or English.

Only Latin.

(19)

Good morning, Mrs. Arthur. Who is ill?

It's my daughter, Dr. Brown.

Let me examine her.

Please come in, doctor.

(After medical examination)

She's got a bad cold. She'll be all right soon. I'll give you the prescription.

Thank you so much doctor.

(20)

A. Can you please tell me where Mrs.Namita lives?

B. Yes, she lives at 1188, Sector V, Pushp Vihar.

A. Thank you.

B. You are welcome.

(21)

Can you finish the work today?

Sorry, I can't.

Why?

'Cause the material is not available.

All right, we can wait for two days.

That's better.

(22)

Good morning everybody. I 've a good news for all of you.

What's the news?

All our students have passed.

That's really great. Let's celebrate.

(23)

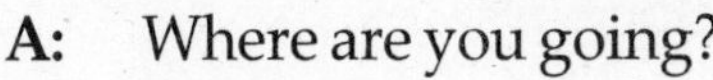

A: Where are you going?

B: I am going to see the fair.

A: Where is it going on?

B: About two kilometres from here.

A: Let me come with you.

B: Yes, you can come with me.

(24)

A. How are you Denis?

B. I am fine. How are you Johan?

A. I am fine too.

I did not see you for a long time.

B. I had gone out on my business tour.

A. Where did you go?

B. To Mumbai.

A. What sort of business do you have?

B. I deal in garments.

(25)

Good morning, sir.

Good morning.

Sir, I'm your student Arthur's brother.

Oh, I see what can I do for you?

Sir, Arthur is not well. Here's his leave application.

What happened?

He's running very high temperature.

All right. Let him take a two days rest.

Thank you, sir.

It's all right.

(26)

Good morning, uncle.

Good morning, Johan. How are you?

I'm fine, uncle.

How is your father?

He is fine too.

Is he at home at present?

Yes, he is.

Please tell him I want to see him.

All right, I'll tell him right now.

(27)

Good morning, uncle.

Good morning, Daniel.

Uncle, may I borrow your car for sometime? I have an urgent work.

Sure, it's there. Take this key.

Thank you so much uncle.

It's all right.

(28)

Is this house for rent?

Yes, it is.

How many bedrooms does it have?

It has three bedrooms.

What is the rent?

It is six hundred and fifty dollars a month.

(29)

Did you enjoy your trip?

Yes, we enjoyed it very much.

How was the scenery?

It was very beautiful.

What beautiful things were there on the way?

There were beautiful trees, fresh flowers and green grass.

(30)

A. What do you want, sir?
B. I want a good plastic emulsion for my house.

A. Which shade, sir?
B. Cream colour.

A. How many tins do you want?
B. Three tins of three litres each.

A. Please wait. Here they are.
B. How much for these?

A. Dollars one hundred and fifty only.
B. Thank you.

A. You are most welcome.

(31)

A. When do you get up?
B. At 7.00 a.m.

A. So late?

B. When do you get up?
A. I get up at 5 o'clock.

B. Why so early?
A. I go for a long walk and do meditation.

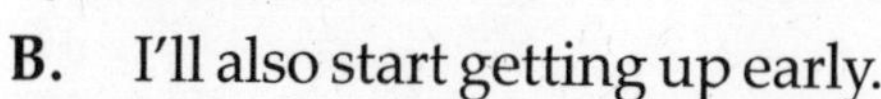

B. I'll also start getting up early.

(32)

Father : Have you done your home work?

Son : I shall do it in the evening.

Father : It is not a good habit to postpone your work. Punctuality is the key to success.

(33)

Are you listening to the teacher?

Yes, I am.

Is the lesson interesting?

Yes, it is.

Are all the students paying attention?

Yes, they are.

(34)

What time is it?

It is half past nine.

Is your watch right?

No, it is five minutes fast.

(35)

What time is it?

It is seven o'clock.

What is Ms. Darcy doing?

She is making breakfast for her family.

What time does her husband leave for office?

He leaves for office at eight o'clock.

(36)

What time do you get up?

I get up at six thirty?

What time do the children get up?

They get up at seven o'clock.

What time does Mr. Wilson get up?

He gets up at seven thirty?

When does Mr. Wilson have breakfast?

He has breakfast at eight o'clock.

(37)

Robert, meet my brother, Johan.

Grace, this is my brother, Johan.

Glad to meet you Johan.

What do you do Johan?

I study in XI standard.

That is very good.

(38)

Excuse me, your face looks familiar to me.

Are you Ms. Darcy?

No, no, I'm his brother, Arthur.

You resemble your brother so closely!

Yes, we are twins.

Really, great!

(39)

Hello, Ralf. How are you?

I'm fine. How about you?

I'm fine too.

I don't find you around these days?

Yes, I'm busy writing some assignments.

What assignments?

My research assignments.

Oh, that is great.

I'm in a hurry. See you again.

Bye.

Bye.

(40)

Do you speak English?

Only a little.

Do you know many words?

No, I don't. I know only the important words.

(41)

Does your mother speak English?

Well she speaks a little English.

Do your sisters speak English?

Yes, they do. They speak it very well.

(42)

What do you usually do in the afternoon?

I usually study or play.

What do you generally do over the weekend?

I generally enjoy sports and visit my friends.

(43)

Do you watch television very often?

Well, I sometimes watch it in the evening.

Did you watch television last night?

Yes, I did. I saw many good programmes.

(44)

Do you watch television very often?

Yes, I do.

How often do you watch television?

I watch it thrice a week.

Does your father watch television?

Yes, he does.

How often does your father watch television?

He watches it once a week.

Do your brothers watch television very often?

Yes, they do.

How often do your brothers watch television?

They watch it five times a week.

(45)

What's a good hotel in this city?

The Taj Mahal Hotel is good.

How far is it from here?

It's quite close—about half a kilometre.

(46)

Where are you staying?

We're staying at an excellent hotel.

What is the name of the hotel?

The Raddison Hotel.

(47)

How long will you be in Delhi?

I'll be here for about one week.

Where are you going to stay?

I am going to stay at Hotel Taj Palace.

(48)

Where's the airline office?

It's near the bus terminal.

How far is that from here?

About half a mile.

(49)

Where's the police station?

It's four blocks that way.

What did you say?

Four blocks up that street.

(50)

Where's the airport?

It's south of the city.

What is the best way to get there?

Take highway 12 to the south.

(51)

What street is the Carlton Hotel?

Sorry, I don't know.

How can I find out?

Please ask a policeman.

(52)

Where do I get the downtown bus?

Walk straight ahead two blocks.

Thanks very much.

You are welcome.

(53)

Where is the bus stop?

At the next corner.

Does any bus go downtown?

Only the number 8 bus goes downtown.

(54)

Are there many bus stops along the street?

Yes, there are. There are quite a few.

Are they located at the corners?

Some of them are, but most of them aren't.

(55)

How do I get to the station?

Take the bus at the next corner.

Do you know which bus I should take?

Watch for number 46.

(56)

Good morning, Darcy.

Good morning. Arthur. How are you?

I'm fine. What about you?

I'm fine too.

That's nice. How do you come here?

I want to meet your manager for an urgent piece of work.

I see.

(57)

When did you come back?

I came yesterday evening.

How was the trip?

It was wonderful.

Did you see the Taj Mahal?

Of course! It's wonderful.

Where else did you go?

I went to Ajmer.

(58)

Was she there at the party?

Yes, she was very much there.

How do you know?

I saw her myself.

But I didn't see.

(59)

Did it rain yesterday?

Yes, it did. That's why it's fine today.

You are right. But the day before it was very hot.

(60)

Is Derick going to have a party?

Yes, he is.

Are his friends and cousins going to come?

Yes, they are.

Is the party going to be next Sunday?

No, it isn't.

Are you going to buy him a gift?

Yes, I am.

Is he going to be fourteen year old.

No, he isn't.

Where is the party going to be?

It's going to be at Derick's house.

What time is party going to be?

It's going to be at seven o'clock.

(61)

When did you have lunch last afternoon?

We had it at two o'clock.

How did you fare in the examination?

Quite well, by the grace of God.

(62)

How long did you work in that hospital?

For about 25 years.

Did you stay there while you worked?

Yes, I did.

(63)

Didn't you do your home work yesterday?

Who told you that?

Your English teacher.

Where did he meet you?

In the market.

It's true. I really didn't do it.

Why?

I forgot.

Do it just now.

(64)

When did you get his letter?

Last Thursday.

Why didn't you reply then?

I was busy at the workshop.

You were, but now you are not.

Yes, now I can.

Do it then, Hurry up.

(65)

Where will he meet me?

He'll meet you at the Railway station.

All right. I'll reach there at 9 sharp.

That'll be fine. Suppose, he gets late?

No problem. I'll spend my time at the Railway platform.

(66)

Where will we have the meeting this time?

We'll have it at Hotel Taj Palace.

How big is the meeting hall there?

It'll accommodate all our 80 delegates.

Are you sure?

Yes, I'm quite sure.

Will there be a break?

Yes, by 1 o'clock.

That's nice.

(67)

Sir, won't (will not) we get any holiday?

Who told you that?

Some employees.

Listen, you all shall get a holiday tomorrow.

(68)

Is it 2689467?

That's right. Who's on the line please?

I am Arthur. Could I speak to Lesley?

One moment.

(after sometime)

She's just gone out. You can leave a message.

Kindly tell her to reach my place by 8 p.m.

Fine.

Could I know your name please?

I am Darcy, her sister.

So nice. Bye Darcy.

Bye Arthur.

Bye.

(69)

Did she come here yesterday?

No she didn't. But she said, she would.

I think Ms. Darcy might have called her.

You may be right. Ms. Darcy was asking for her last Monday.

(70)

Could/Would you do me a favour, please?

It'd be my pleasure.

Please give this letter to Derick.

Sure.

Thank you.

You are most welcome.

(71)

Could you connect me to room No. 506?

Sure, sir. Please hold on.

(After a few seconds)

Sir, no one is picking up the phone.

All right, you may please try after about ten minutes and let me know.

Fine sir.

Thank you.

You are welcome.

(72)

My friend can speak French.

Arthur can too.

But my friend can't speak German.

Alice can't either.

(73)

We went to the cinema last night.

We did too.

But we didn't get there on time.

We didn't either.

(74)

I met Johan in his office.

So did I.

But I didn't meet his secretary.

Neither did I.

(75)

They are going to the concert today.

I am too.

They are also going to the National Park.

So am I.

(76)

We've already solved the sums.

So have we.

But we haven't checked the answers.

Neither have we.

(77)

Are you going to attend the party?

Yes, I am.

Are you going to stay very late?

No, I 'm not.

(78)

Will Arthur be at the party?

Yes, he will, but he'll be a little late.

Will he be with his weekend guests.

No, he won't.

(79)

Have you ever been to the National Museum?

No, I never have.

Would you care to go there with me tomorrow?

Yes, I certainly would.

(80)

Don't you work every Saturday morning?

No, we don't. Just on occasion.

Did you work last Saturday morning?

No, we didn't.

(81)

Are you going to your office now?

No I'm not, but I'll be leaving shortly.

Do you go to office everyday?

No, I don't, only five days in a week.

(82)

When did the Peters take a trip to Scotland?

They took it last summer.

Whom did they visit?

They visited Mr. Arthur's parents.

When did they leave?

They left on Sunday morning.

How long did they stay?

They stayed for three weeks.

(83)

Did you eat breakfast early?

Yes, I did.

Did Mr. Peter go to the filling station?

Yes, he did.

Did Mr. Peter buy new tyres for the trip?

No, he didn't.

Did they stay in Scotland for four weeks?

No, they didn't.

(84)

When do you have your vacation?

In May and June.

Does it last for two months?

No, my vacation is for six weeks.

(85)

Where are you going now?

To the airport.

Are you going by bus or by train?

Probably by taxi, if I can get one.

(86)

Are you Dr. Robin?

No. That tall fellow is Dr. Robin.

Do you mean the one over there with glasses?

Yes, the one with brown hair.

(87)

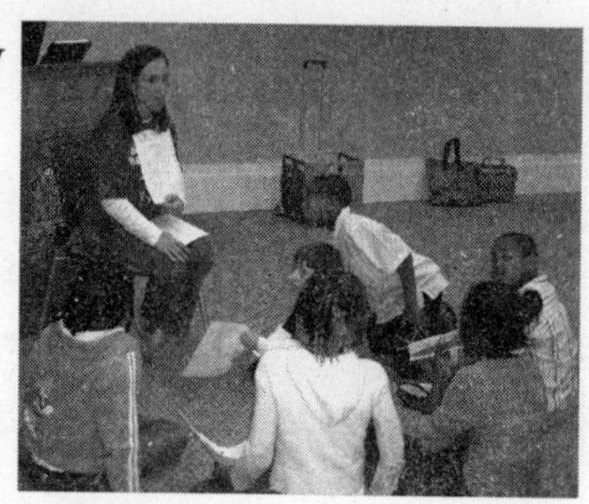

When does February have twenty nine days?

In a leap year.

How often is there a leap year?

Every fourth year.

(88)

How many days are there in a leap year?

There are three hundred and sixty six days.

How many weeks are there in a year?

There are fifty two weeks in a year.

(89)

What floor is your apartment on?

It's on the fourth floor?

Is the building a walk-up?

No, it has a small elevator.

(90)

Is this your apartment?

Yes, it is.

How many bedrooms do you have?

Three big ones and one small one.

(91)

What would you like to see?

I'd like to see your overcoats, please.

What kind of overcoats would you like to see?

I'd like to see your winter overcoats.

(92)

Did you sell your car?

Yes, I sold it to my friend Cratchet.

Did you put the money in the bank?

I deposited part of it and spent the rest.

(93)

Do you want to learn English?

Yes, I do.

Why do you want to learn English?

Because it'll be useful in my future?

(94)

What are you studying right now?

I'm doing my English assignment.

What is the toughest thing about English?

Pronunciation is the toughest thing for me.

(95)

Where did you get that book?

From the library in my neighbourhood.

Is it a good library?

Of course, it is.

(96)

Where is Mr. Johan?

He's in the other office right now.

Do you expect him back soon?

Yes, I do, in just a few minutes.

(97)

Would you like to see some pictures?

Sure. Did you take them yourself?

Yes, I did. I've got a new camera.

Pictures are really wonderful.

(98)

I'd like to speak to Mr. Arthur.

Sorry. He isn't in now.

Can I leave a message for him?

Yes. I'll take the message.

(99)

Someone wants to talk to you on the telephone?

Who is it? Do you know?

I'm sorry. I forgot to ask.

It's all right. I think I know who it is.

(100)

What's the matter?

I'm worried about something.

What's wrong?

I think I have lost my wallet.

ANSWERS

EXERCISE 1

1. Boy
2. Woman
3. Hole
4. Cat
5. Fan
6. Apple
7. Ball
8. Dog
9. Egg
10. Bed

EXERCISE 2

1. He is a good boy.
2. I have lost the pen which you gave me.
3. Darcy is an honest girl.
4. There is an inkpot on the table.
5. I waited for you for an hour.
6. She is an honourable woman.
7. I met a European in the party.
8. How beautiful the sky looks!
9. Gold is a precious metal.
10. He has come without an umbrella.

EXERCISE 3

1.	The tiger is in the cage.	Assertive
2.	Please bring a glass of water.	Imperative
3.	Don't make a noise.	Imperative
4.	May you be blessed with a son!	Optative
5.	Hurrah! we have won the series.	Exclamatory
6.	Alas! her only son is dead.	Exclamatory
7.	Listen to the speech attentively.	Imperative
8.	Where do you live?	Interrogative
9.	She is plucking flowers.	Assertive

10.	He goes to office everyday.	Assertive
11.	He has returned my books.	Assertive
12.	The child has been crying since morning.	Assertive
13.	The brave soldier lost an arm in the battle.	Assertive
14.	Show me your home work.	Imperative
15.	Where are you going?	Interrogative
16.	Do not violate the rules.	Imperative
17.	May you live long!	Optative
18.	Do you play cricket?	Interrogative
19.	Where has he gone?	Interrogative
20.	What a wonderful weather!	Exclamatory
21.	She can solve these sums.	Assertive
22.	I was treated well by all.	Assertive
23.	Lift this box.	Imperative
24.	Come here.	Imperative
25.	What a shameful act!	Exclamatory

EXERCISE 4

1. I have seen this movie.
2. Mother is making tea.
3. All know him.
4. Children fly kites on the Republic Day.
5. The maid-servant has washed the clothes.
6. We heard a barking sound.
7. The saint sat on the hill.
8. Students have completed their homework.

EXERCISE 5

1. The hunter chased the rabbit.

2. My father works in a private company.
3. The French Army fought bravely.
4. Practice and experience make a man perfect.
5. He is a noble person.
6. The peon rang the bell.
7. The children are playing in the park.
8. Manners reveal character.

EXERCISE 6

1.	That he will come in time.	Clause
2.	If they had reached there.	Clause
3.	All are born to suffer.	Sentence
4.	Man is mortal.	Sentence
5.	In the air.	Phrase
6.	To learn driving	Phrase
7.	Although he is rich.	Clause
8.	With a long tail.	Phrase
9.	To carry out the work.	Phrase
10.	He climbed.	Sentence

EXERCISE 7

This	cat	these	cats
This	jug	these	jugs
This	table	these	tables
This	garden	these	gardens
This	flower	these	flowers

EXERCISE 8

This	ball	These	balls
This	house	These	houses

This	apple	These	apples
This	girl	These	girls
This	pen	These	pens
This	table	These	tables

EXERCISE 9

1.	Man	(Common Noun)
	Village	(Common Noun)
2.	Taj Mahal	(Proper Noun)
	Agra	(Proper Noun)
3.	Soldier	(Common Noun)
	Award	(Common Noun)
4.	Health	(Abstract Noun)
	Happiness	(Abstract Noun)
5.	Honesty	(Abstract Noun)
	Policy	(Abstract Noun)
6.	Bouquet	(Collective Noun)
	Birthday	(Abstract Noun)
7.	Crowd	(Collective Noun)
	Stones	(Common Noun)
	Policemen	(Common Noun)
8.	Delhi	(Proper Noun)
	Capital	(Common Noun)
	India	(Proper Noun)
9.	Bunch	(Collective Noun)
	Keys	(Common Noun)
	Bus	(Common Noun)
10.	Cleanliness	(Abstract Noun)
	Godliness	(Abstract Noun)

EXERCISE 10

1. Lion	lioness
2. Cock-sparrow	hen-sparrow
3. Ox	cow
4. Gander	goose
5. Author	authoress
6. Baron	baroness
7. Host	hostess
8. Count	countess
9. Duke	duchess
10. Buck	doe
11. Colt	filly
12. Ram	ewe
13. Heir	heiress
14. Negro	negress
15. Prince	princess
16. Waiter	waitress
17. Peacock	peahen
18. Tiger	tigress
19. Son	daughter
20. Father	mother

EXERCISE 11

1. Mango	mangoes
2. Bird	birds
3. Class	classes
4. Branch	branches
5. Buffalo	buffaloes
6. Potato	potatoes
7. Woman	women

8. Foot	feet
9. Maid servant	maid-servants
10. Son-in law	sons in law
11. Knife	knives
12. Story	stories
13. Baby	babies
14. Dish	dishes
15. Volcano	volcanoes
16. Cargo	cargoes
17. Mouse	mice
18. Tooth	teeth
19. Child	children
20. Shelf	shelves
21. Step daughter	step-daughters
22. Commander-in-Chief	commanders-in-chief
23. Looker on	lookers on
24. Calf	calves
25. Goose	geese

EXERCISE 12

1. This is the book which he gave me.
2. He is the boy who stood first in the class.
3. He knew what you meant.
4. He is the person whom we can trust.
5. Teachers like the students who work hard.
6. Do you know what has happened?
7. No man can lose that he never got.
8. He has gone to Delhi which is his birthplace.
9. This is the instrument which they installed.
10. These are the boys who have been selected for awards.

11. This is the pen that I got as a prize.
12. I saw the snake which bit the cow.
13. You cannot have what you don't deserve.
14. Darcy got back the money which she had lost.
15. This is the gift which I have selected for you.

EXERCISE 13

1. The storm caused heavy damage to the ship.
   Heavy— Adjective of Quality
2. She is an old and weak woman
   (i) Old— Adjective of Quality
   (ii) Weak— Adjective of Quality.
3. There are many errors in your essay.
   Many— Adjective of Number
4. Every man must do his duty.
   Every— Distributive Adjective
5. Which book did you select?
   Which— Interrogative Adjective
6. I have three ball point pens
   three— Adjective Number
7. He died a heroic death
   Heroic— Adjective of Quality
8. Honest and sincere persons win in the last stage.
   (i) Honest— Adjective of Quality
   (ii) Sincere— Adjective of Quality
   (iii) Last— Adjective of Number

EXERCISE 14

1. It was a huge building.
2. I saw a big snake in the forest.

3. The first prize was won by the Indian.
4. The great man lives in a small hut.
5. She brought ripe mangoes.
6. I like fresh food.
7. My mother cooks tasty breakfast.
8. The wise persons seek his advice.
9. Sita was a devoted wife.
10. She is the woman of high ambition.

EXERCISE 15

		Adjective
1.	Happiness	Happy
2.	Hope	Hopeful/ Hopeless
3.	Heaviness	Heavy
4.	Sickness	Sick
5.	Child	Childish
6.	Boy	Boyish
7.	Woman	Womanly
8.	Peace	Peaceful
9.	Joy	Joyful
10.	Quarrel	Quarrelsome
11.	Friend	Friendly
12.	Ambition	Ambitious
13.	Sorrow	Sorrowful
14.	Laughter	Laughable
15.	Wonder	Wonderful

EXERCISE 16

		Comparative Degree	Superlative Degree
1.	Brave	*Braver*	*Bravest*

2. Heavy	*Heavier*	*Heaviest*
3. Beautiful	*more beautiful*	*most beautiful*
4. Ugly	*uglier*	*ugliest*
5. Noisy	*noisier*	*noisiest*
6. Timid	*more timid*	*most timid*
7. Wise	*wiser*	*wisest*
8. Noble	*nobler*	*noblest*
9. Large	*larger*	*largest*
10. Happy	*happier*	*happiest*
11. Easy	*easier*	*easiest*
12. Hot	*hotter*	*hottest*
13. Thin	*thinner*	*thinnest*
14. Small	*smaller*	*smallest*
15. Young	*younger*	*youngest*

EXERCISE 17

1. *Better* – Comparative Degree of Adjective
2. *Best* – Superlative Degree of Adjective
3. *(i) Less* – Comparative Degree of Adjective
   (ii) Hot – Positive Degree of Adjective
4. *Idlest* – Superlative Degree of Adjective
5. *(i) Unhappy* – Positive Degree of Adjective
   (ii) Happier – Comparative Degree of Adjective
6. *Highest* – Superlative Degree of Adjective
7. *Hot* – Positive Degree of Adjective
8. *Mild* – Positive Degree of Adjective
9. *Best* – Superlative Degree of Adjective
10. *Untidy* – Positive Degree of Adjective

EXERCISE 18

1. Are you feeling better today?

2. June is hotter than any other month.
3. Silver is cheaper than gold.
4. Common people are the best judge.
5. Arthur's work is bad, Daniel's is worse, but yours is the worst.
6. This is the most beautiful area.
7. These are the best mangoes.
8. You are the best friend, I know.
9. My doll is better than yours.
10. The Himalayas are the highest mountains in the world.

EXERCISE 19

Present	Past	Past Participle
Write	*wrote*	*written*
Read	*read*	*read*
Speak	*spoke*	*spoken*
Bathe	*bathed*	*bathed*
Know	*knew*	*known*
Tell	*told*	*told*
Hear	*heard*	*heard*
Play	*played*	*played*
Put	*put*	*put*
Feel	*felt*	*felt*
Cut	*cut*	*cut*
Breed	*bred*	*bred*
Shut	*shut*	*shut*
Creep	*crept*	*crept*
Spread	*spread*	*spread*
Lose	*lost*	*lost*
Dance	*danced*	*danced*
Give	*gave*	*given*

Go	*went*	*gone*
Come	*came*	*come*
Grow	*grew*	*grown*
Hide	*hid*	*hid/hidden*
Forget	*forgot*	*forgotten*
Fly	*flew*	*flown*
Flow	*flowed*	*flowed*
Find	*found*	*found*
Get	*got*	*got*
Choose	*chose*	*chosen*
Begin	*began*	*begun*
Beat	*beat*	*beaten*
Arise	*arose*	*arisen*
Bear	*bore*	*borne*
Kneel	*knelt*	*knelt*
Win	*won*	*won*
Blow	*blew*	*blown*
Become	*became*	*become*
Tear	*tore*	*torn*
Sell	*sold*	*sold*
Teach	*taught*	*taught*
Learn	*learnt*	*learnt*
Buy	*bought*	*bought*
Bring	*brought*	*brought*
Catch	*caught*	*caught*
Seek	*sought*	*sought*
Refuse	*refused*	*refused*
Make	*made*	*made*
Telecast	*telecast*	*telecast*

Broadcast	*broadcast*	*broadcast*
Lend	*lent*	*lent*
Quit	*quit*	*quit*
Smell	*smelt*	*smelt*
Spend	*spent*	*spent*
Think	*thought*	*thought*
Weep	*wept*	*wept*
Burst	*burst*	*burst*
Hurt	*hurt*	*hurt*
Let	*let*	*let*
Meet	*met*	*met*
Pay	*paid*	*paid*
Say	*said*	*said*
Sing	*sang*	*sung*
See	*saw*	*seen*
Hold	*held*	*held*
Ring	*rang*	*rung*
Run	*ran*	*run*
Shoot	*shot*	*shot*
Shine	*shone*	*shone*
Shake	*shook*	*shaken*
Shrink	*shrank*	*shrunk*
Strive	*strove*	*striven*
Take	*took*	*taken*
Swear	*swore*	*sworn*
Throw	*threw*	*thrown*
Swim	*swam*	*swum*
Wear	*wore*	*worn*
Build	*built*	*built*

Feed	*fed*	*fed*
Have	*had*	*had*
Carry	*carried*	*carried*

EXERCISE 20

1. *met* — *Main Verb*
2. (i) *were* — *Auxiliary Verb*
   (ii) *flying* — *Main Verb*
3. (i) *did* — *Auxiliary Verb*
   (ii) *return* — *Main Verb*
4. (i) *are* — *Auxiliary Verb*
   (ii) *dancing* — *Main Verb*
5. (i) *does* — *Auxiliary Verb*
   (ii) *like* — *Main verb*
6. (i) *Shall be* — *Auxiliary Verb*
   (ii) *getting* — *Main Verb*
7. (i) *have* — *Auxiliary Verb*
   (ii) *downed* — *Main Verb*
8. (i) *are* — *Auxiliary Verb*
   (ii) *chasing* — *Main Verb*
9. *waters* — *Main Verb*
10. *lost* — *Main Verb*

EXERCISE 21

1. *is sleeping* — Intransitive verb
2. *brought* — Transitive verb
3. *fly* — Intransitive verb
4. *struck* — Transitive verb
5. *know* — Transitive verb
6. *read* — Transitive verb

7. *roared* — Transitive verb
8. *played* — Transitive verb

EXERCISE 22

1. She spoke *softly*.
2. This player runs *fast*.
3. He *often* visits this place.
4. You have been *badly* treated.
5. The boy hit the ball *strongly*.
6. He slipped and fell *down*.
7. She is a *very* intelligent girl.
8. His condition is *much* worse today.
9. This boy can *never* steal anything.
10. The soldiers fought *bravely*.
11. Don't go *there*.
12. *Luckily* everyone escaped unhurt.

EXERCISE 23

1. I came early.
2. She closed the door angrily.
3. The boys fared well in the examination.
4. She sang well.
5. Don't go out.
6. I can hardly believe it.
7. The girl is very shy.
8. He left the house late today.
9. I don't decide anything hurriedly.
10. The principal spoke softly.
11. You should always aim high.
12. We can easily guess.

13. The patient is much better.
14. He often comes to our house.
15. The children ran fast.

EXERCISE 24

1. She was sitting *beside* her daughter (beside)
2. The cat is sitting *in* the corner. (in)
3. The lion and the unicorn fought *for* the crown. (for)
4. The Piper stopped *into* the street (into)
5. They all ran *after* the dacoit's wife (after)
6. Such a number of rocks came *over* his head. (over)
7. The village smith stands *under* a spreading chestnut tree. (under)
8. He goes *to* the church on Sundays and sits *among* his boys. (to, among)
9. She is fond *of* architecture (of)
10. It is natural *in* everyman *to* wish *for* distinction (in, to, for)
11. The goat subsists *on* the coarsest *of* food. (on, of)
12. He proved quite a match *for* the giant. (for)
13. India is teeming *with* natural wealth. (with)
14. Jaunpur is famous *for* its perfumes. (for)
15. This tree is associated *with* scenes *of* goodwill and rejoicing. (with, of)

EXERCISE 25

1. Do not cry over spilt milk.
2. They motored from Mumbai to Goa.
3. I shall do it with pleasure.
4. The river flows under the bridge.
5. The dog ran across the road.

6. The robber jumped over the compound wall.
7. The soldier died for his country.
8. The child is afraid of the dog.
9. The work was done in haste.
10. The property was destroyed in fire.
11. She has known me for a long time.
12. The moon does not shine with its own light.
13. She has not yet recovered from illness.
14. We started at six in the morning.
15. Since last year I have seen him but once.

EXERCISE 26

1. He will not succeed *unless* he works harder. (unless)
2. She arrived *after* you had gone. (after)
3. We waited *till* the bus arrived. (till)
4. Bread *and* milk is wholesome food. (and)
5. He will get the prize *if* he deserves. (if)
6. *When* you are called, you must come at once. (when)
7. Do not go *before* mother comes. (before)
8. *Since* you say so, I must believe it. (since)
9. The soldier fled *lest* he should be killed. (lest)
10. He did not come *because* you did not call him. (because)
11. He is richer *than* I (am). (than)
12. I will stay *until* he returns. (until)

EXERCISE 27

1. Be just and fear not.
2. He ran fast, but he missed the train.
3. They fled, because they were afraid.

4. Make haste or you will be late.
5. I am sure that she said so.
6. Wait till he returns.
7. You finished first though you began late.
8. Since he was ambitious, I slew him.
9. If you eat too much, you will be ill.
10. Arthur is slow but sure.

EXERCISE 28

1. Two and two make four.
2. Is her name Darcy or Lesley?
3. I shall not go if it rains.
4. Unless you run, you will not overtake him.
5. You should not go now as it is raining very heavily.
6. You will not get the prize unless you deserve.
7. She told me that you had arrived an hour ago.
8. She is very rich but she is not happy.
9. Water and oil will not mix.
10. She left before we returned.

EXERCISE 29

1. My father is well but my mother is ill.
2. He sells bananas and he sells mangoes.
3. I did not succeed though I worked hard.
4. We honor him because he is a brave man.
5. Although he is poor, he is honest.
6. Although she is rich, she is not happy.
7. I sat down because I was tired.
8. Boys must be quiet or they must leave the room.
9. Arthur neither came nor did he send a letter.

10. The leaves are falling because it is autumn.
11. Although he tried his best he lost the prize.
12. You may go but I will stay.

EXERCISE 30

1. Present Perfect Continuous
2. Simple Present
3. Present Continuous
4. Simple Present
5. Present Perfect
6. Simple Present
7. Simple Present
8. Present Continuous
9. Present Perfect Continuous
10. Present Perfect Continuous

EXERCISE 31

1. Past Simple
2. Past Continuous
3. (i) Past Perfect (ii) Perfect Past
4. Past Continuous
5. (i) Past Perfect (ii) Perfect Past
6. Past Simple
7. Past Continuous
8. (i) Past Perfect (ii) Perfect Past
9. Past Simple
10. Past Simple

EXERCISE 32

1. Future Continuous
2. Future Perfect
3. Simple Future
4. Simple Future

5. Future Perfect Continuous
6. Future Continuous
7. Simple Future
8. Future Continuous
9. Future Continuous
10. Simple Future

EXERCISE 33

1. He does not come here regularly.
2. This dog does not bark very loudly.
3. The sun has not set.
4. The boys have not been working since morning.
5. I do not play hockey.
6. He has not collected his salary.
7. She doesn't speak softly.
8. They are not disturbing us.
9. He does not care for the poor.
10. Girls are not dancing.

EXERCISE 34

1. Does she know you?
2. Has the teacher finished his lecture?
3. Are they solving the sums?
4. Do I enjoy myself at their place?
5. Has the child been crying since morning?
6. Is the girl playing with her dolls?
7. Has the examiner sealed all the question papers?
8. Does she speak fluent English?
9. Is the hawker selling bangles?
10. Has she been working in this office for ten years?

EXERCISE 35

1. I did not write her two letters.
2. She had not typed all the letters when the managing director came.
3. They did not spread the rumour.
4. The boys were not learning their lessons.
5. This team did not score three goals.
6. We had not reached the airport when the rain started.
7. Children did not fly many kites on Independence Day.
8. Girls had not been dancing since morning.

EXERCISE 36

1. Did the farmers sow the seeds?
2. Had they not reached the office when the rain started?
3. Did the peon ring the bell?
4. Were they watching the match?
5. Did storm fell many trees?
6. Were girls making clay models?
7. Had he been working for six hours?

EXERCISE 37

1. I shall not take rest.
2. He will not carry out the work.
3. The tutor will not be teaching me tomorrow.
4. He will not have been speaking for one hour.
5. I shall not have completed my work by evening.
6. The farmers will not be ploughing their fields.

EXERCISE 38

1. Will they go for a walk?
2. Will the pilot take off at 7 a.m.?
3. Will the farmers have ploughed their fields?

4. Will the warriors fight a duel?
5. Will mother knit a sweater?
6. Will he have been studying since morning?
7. Will the tailor have stitched your uniform by tomorrow?
8. Will all the players receive awards?

EXERCISE 39

1. I met him at the party yesterday.
2. She has been learning English for two years.
3. He knows me for a long time.
4. The sun rises in the east.
5. She has written me only two letters up to now.
6. My father left ten minutes ago.
7. This magazine appears once in a week.
8. My uncle will arrive next week.
9. I have not met my friend this week.
10. Boys are learning their lessons now.
11. Do you know him?
12. Has he been working since morning?
13. We had reached home when the rain started.
14. The train will have left when we reach the station.
15. The children fly kites on Independence Day.
16. My father usually comes home at 9 p.m; but he has not come yet.

EXERCISE 40

1. The kite *flew* in the sky.
2. The girls *sang* sweetly.
3. Arthur *came* of a good family.
4. Birds *were* singing.
5. My friend *wrote* to me every month.
6. This person *swam* very well.

7. The teacher *punished* the guilty students.
8. I had been *waiting* for him for a long time.
9. He *came* home very late.
10. Girls *were making* clay models.
11. Darcy *knew* her work very well.
12. He *had been* sleeping for a long time.
13. He *forgot* my name.
14. I *went* for a morning walk every day.
15. He *made* clay models.

EXERCISE 41

1. He *makes* many mistakes in his essay.
2. He *knows* me.
3. I *write* to my mother every week.
4. The coward soldier *flees* from the battlefield.
5. A small stroke *fells* great oaks.
6. Your gum *bleeds* profusely.
7. She *cuts* the vegetables.
8. This child *flies* many kites.
9. She *drinks* the milk very fast.
10. All people *hold* him in high esteem.
11. He *knows* his job well.
12. The sun is *shining* brightly.
13. People are *taking* a morning walk.
14. She *forgets* all I tell her.
15. It *takes* three days to reach Chennai.

EXERCISE 42

See : I saw him at the party yesterday.
She saw this movie last month.

Begin	:	The movie had begun when he reached the cinema hall.
		The match began at 10 a.m.
		He began to speak nuisance after consuming alcohol.
Run	:	On seeing the tiger, he ran for his life.
		He had run five kilometers when we reached the spot.
Tear	:	In a fit of anger he tore the letter.
		His shirt was torn.
		He is mentally torn.
Catch	:	The thief was caught by the police.
		I caught sight of a new animal in the zoo.
		They caught fish.
Give	:	The teacher has given us a test.
		I gave him a beautiful present on his birthday.
		He never gave them a chance to speak.
Steal	:	Her purse was stolen by this man.
		The burglars stole money from the almirah.
		His heart was stolen by her.
Sow	:	One must reap what one has sown.
		The farmer sowed the seeds.
Write	:	He has written this essay.
		I wrote him a letter yesterday.
Eat	:	Lunch was eaten in haste.
		He ate his dinner on time.
Say	:	Who said these words?
		I have said what I wanted to say.
Fly	:	Where has the bird flown?
		Many birds flew in the sky.

Find : Who has found my pen?

I have found the right answer.

Shoot : Who shot the tiger?

The poachers shot down the elephant.

Teacher : Who taught you English last year?

The teacher has already taught this lesson.

EXERCISE 43

1. I don't think I (*shall*, should, can) be able to go.
2. She (shall, *will*, dare) not pay unless compelled.
3. You (*should*, would, ought) be punctual.
4. I wish you (should, *would*, must) tell me earlier.
5. (*Shall*, will, would) I assist you?
6. (Shall, should, *would*) you please help me with this?
7. One (*ought*, should, must) to pay one's debts.
8. He said I (can, *might*, should) use his mobile phone any time.
9. If you (shall, *should*, would) see her, give her my regards.
10. She (need, *dare*, would) not ask for a raise for fear of losing her job.
11. I (needn't to see, needn't have seen, *didn't need to see*) her, so I sent a letter.
12. (shall, might, *could*) you show me the way to the station?
13. To save his life, he *ran* fast; and (would, could, *was able to*) reach safely.
14. She (would, *used*, ought) to be an atheist but she believes in God.
15. You (needn't, *mustn't*, won't) light a match, the room is full of gas.

16. is to
17. didn't need to wait.
18. might
19. will
20. would
21. would
22. was to have left
23. used to
24. shall
25. might

NOTES

NOTES

NOTES

NOTES